THE COMPLETE HOME SECURITY GUIDE

A particularly well presented home with prominent and secure physical automatic swing gates and an access control system. It has an open aspect so concealment by intruders around the perimeter of the house is difficult. Lighting is reassuring and a remote lockable post box is installed. The intercom deters bogus callers as they are retained at the outskirts of the home and have to seek permission to enter through the gates. A gravel drive allows the occupants to hear any approach to the property and hinders 'sneak thieves'. This all suggests to the casual observer that the home owner is vigilant and is prepared to invest in security, and that there is a high probability that further security features will be present.

THE COMPLETE HOME SECURITY GUIDE

Gerard Honey

THE CROWOOD PRESS

First published in 2012 by
The Crowood Press Ltd
Ramsbury, Marlborough
Wiltshire SN8 2HR

www.crowood.com

British Library Cataloguing-in-Publication Data
A catalogue record for this book is available from the British Library.

ISBN 978 1 84797 397 9

Acknowledgements
The author would like to thank all of those who provided information for this book and in particular: Aldridge Security, B. Rourke & Co. Ltd, ExecEngineers, FAAC (UK) Ltd, Honeywell, JWM Control Systems, Metropolitan Police Service, Osram UK, Panasonic, Pyronix, Roche Systems Ltd and *The Locksmith* magazine.

Typeset by Bookcraft Ltd, Stroud, Gloucestershire
Printed and bound in India by Replika Press Pvt Ltd

Contents

Introduction

We live in times where security is becoming an even greater priority as a means of protecting ourselves and our property and possessions. Certainly both crime prevention and security within the domestic environment are closely allied in terms of managing and controlling the risks with which we are faced. For certain, it is vital that we are safe and secure when we are actually within the confines of our own home, but we must also have effective protection in place for those occasions when our property is vacant. It is important for our sense of well-being that we can always feel confident in the measures we have taken to safeguard ourselves and our property at all times.

In real terms we are all vulnerable to some extent, since the existence of crime makes us all potential victims. This applies to all forms of house types and architecture, so the role of security and protection is a serious one, no matter which environment we live in; this may be communal or remote rural living, as we must pay equal attention to all residential groups and their surrounding areas. Indeed, Home Office sources indicate that without any basic home security we are all ten times more likely to be burgled.

As a means of satisfying all homeowners, this book makes reference to police initiatives and official standards and governing body requirements, as appropriate, to every form of domestic residence. Furthermore it is written at a level that is understandable and can therefore be used by any reader with an interest in any form of domestic security policy and yet it is able to extend its appeal to include planners and architects.

We can therefore claim that this book is indeed an overall and essential guide to domestic security and crime prevention, since it is wide in scope being both informative and practical. It includes many tables that can be used for guidance as to how we need to approach and address all of the security problems that continue to face us on a daily basis. These tables illustrate, in a clear format, the range of security issues that are dealt with in this book. Further, in its presentation this work uses a broad range of informative text, diagrams and photographs for illustrative purposes, so as to show exactly how all of the various security functions are applied in the real world. It has also been the aim to make the book interesting to read by reflecting on real-world issues that have been gathered over the years from various parties involved with security.

The content of *The Complete Home Security Guide* has been compiled in the first instance to illustrate how we can establish a risk assessment for our property, taking into account the standard procedures and sequence of events. Following that initial stage, which deals with the classification of risk, we can then move on to consider the primary issues of burglary prevention, alongside the requirements of the insurance industry and how to deal with bogus callers to our home.

In the next stage of the book we give consideration as to how we can apply perimeter protection and boundaries by natural methods, such as hedging and foliage. From this we are then able to move on to other physical security methods to include gates and barriers allied to the full range of mechanical locking devices, together with purely visible deterrents.

Developing our knowledge further, the next methods of managing risk are devoted to electronic security systems, such as intruder alarms, together with door entry and intercoms used as access control technologies. Fire and carbon monoxide detection are included as necessary security issues. Monitoring our property by observation and CCTV systems from local or remote locations is then discussed.

Lighting forms our next topic as we detail the different lighting forms and illumination levels and fittings appropriate to the risk, and the best means of selecting the lighting for any given application or location. This includes lighting for both external use and internal schemes.

Moving on a stage we detail how notification or signalling is applied so as to notify any activity or indeed intrusion within the protected home. This may be by sound or by silent notification or picture evidence to nominated persons. We even relay information on the application of such innovative practices as home automation security and the integration of a variety of systems into one collective unit. Miscellaneous components for home security are also included at the end of this chapter covering such things as small, self-

contained, inexpensive and easily fitted devices. Checklists and planning, together with Building Regulations and Local Authority requirements, are formed towards the end of the book into an essential data collection for reference purposes. These include an overall checklist and planning sheet to cover our essential security and a short checklist for when we go away on holiday. We complete our investigations with some case studies that represent real-world home security applications, things to think about if we move to a different home and then how to budget for our security issues.

Included is a short glossary that can be used as a quick reference aid to obtain definitions or expanded explanations of some of the major areas and technologies that are contained in this book. A list of useful contacts with sources of information completes the chapter alongside information on coping with a burglary.

In practice this book exists in order to fulfil many purposes in relation to domestic security. Indeed the duty of *The Complete Home Security Guide* is to place all of the recognized security policies and systems into a single and definitive source, in a clearly defined and easily understood way. Following this, the policies and systems, which are then able to be put into place by the user, can evolve from what has been a truly effective risk analysis.

chapter one

The Home Risk Assessment

In this, the first chapter, we are going to look at the home risk assessment because it is the results of this that very much identify the risks that we and our property face in relation to all security issues. Having completed this stage we will then be able to look at the ways in which we can develop risk-reduction measures and implement them in a practical way. Disclosure of information is also an important subject as we do not want to compromise the security measures we already have or intend to implement. Therefore, information must be retained in a secure way.

Risk assessment for various issues is something we are all facing in a number of ways but the expression 'risk assessment' is a very generic term. We hear about it in the course of our work and even when we go on holiday, so what are the reasons for a risk assessment and what does it involve, we may ask ourselves. Well let us look specifically at the fundamental questions that it relates to with regard to home security.

Q. What is a home risk assessment?

It is a systematic method of looking at all our home security issues and considering the problems with which we could be faced, associated with the individual or property to be protected. This involves loss, damage and injury. The assessment must include the controls needed to eliminate, reduce or minimize the risks.

Q. Why carry out a home risk assessment?

It is a fundamental requirement because if we don't conduct a risk assessment, then we have not determined where the risks are and what dangers we may face. The aim should always be to reduce the risks as far as 'reasonably practicable', the term reasonably practicable being a time-honoured expression used to appraise risk reduction against the degree of risk presented. It must also be the case that the assessment includes a budget associated with any costs that would be incurred to implement the findings.

Q. Who should conduct the home risk assessment?

A competent person should be used. If the homeowner feels confident, then they may carry out the initial risk assessment themselves and from this detail their own findings. These findings can then be submitted for a professional appraisal or be endorsed by a further party in the security industry or by an insurance specialist.

Q. Who should the home risk assessment cover?

All of the security and safety risks posed to all of the individuals in the home and to the property, outbuildings and land that are associated with the home. Also, any other persons who could be affected as a result of being involved with the home in question.

Q. How do we go about assessing the risks?
There can be no hard and fast rules as to how the assessment should be conducted, as everyone will adopt a slightly different approach. However, it is important that the assessment be carried out systematically and all of the foreseeable risks are considered. In general we have a differentiation between hazards and risks:

- Hazards are those factors that have the potential to cause harm or injury.
- Risks are the likelihood that damage or loss can occur and how severe the outcome may be.

We need to identify the hazards and those who may be harmed by those hazards. We need to identify the ways to manage the risks present and decide what additional steps are required to reduce the risks further, which are our control measures.

The findings of the assessment need to be recorded and those at risk advised.

Q. How often should we conduct a home risk assessment?

This should be done annually, although it is always possible to make reviews on a regular basis if there have been any fundamental changes by looking at each aspect as critically as possible.

Q. How do we control the risks?

When deciding on the control measures we must determine if the risks can be avoided or eliminated or how they may at least be contained within a given level.

Q. How detailed should the home risk assessment be?

The level of detail is to relate to the level of risk. Always use basic forms and present the data with checklists so that the required information is easily found and may be clearly understood.

For our own purposes in relation to the security issues we face for the home let us start to look at the procedures and sequence of events that we need to follow.

PROCEDURES AND SEQUENCE OF EVENTS

Let us reiterate that the reader must appreciate exactly what the security home risk assessment is, and how it is intended to be used, before studying the relationships of home security and the various ways in which it can be implemented.

We have already said that the home risk assessment is a method used to identify, in a precise and in a defined way, the risks that are associated with an individual or the property to be protected. The results of this can then be used to bring in measures to minimize the risks that have been found and bring these to an acceptable level in order to deal with those risks. It has to be said that the risk assessment must use standard procedures and follow a recognized sequence of events, if it is to be credible.

In reality we cannot eliminate all of the risks that are continually presented to the security and to the protection of the welfare of homeowners. However, we can reduce those risks to a manageable level by the correct implementation of measures that take away, or at least diminish, all of the problem factors that are associated with the risks we face.

So we must have a process to help us understand the ways we gather information and then have a method by which we can put into effect ways, procedures and systems to deal with the findings of the home risk assessment.

A sequence of events will be that we:

- Carry out the home risk assessment.
- Identify the risks.
- Develop risk-reduction measures.
- Implement the risk-reduction measures.

However, we must do all of this in a practical way and it must all be performed in defined and credible ways that reflect current practices so as to deal with the security issues that surround us. But how do we carry out this home risk assessment?

Although there is no particular method for carrying out the risk assessment, it is necessary to ensure that all risks are considered for the premises, covering the following essential criteria:

- Location.
- Building design.
- Contents of home.

In fact a full description of risk-assessment guidance is contained in the European Standards EN 50131, which are used by the professional security industry. They are adopted as the application guidelines for intruder alarm systems, since they form the nucleus of the electronic security systems division. Therefore we can adopt these for our own needs because of the status they hold.

A number of stages have to be considered. For our own needs we can use this guidance and by doing so adopt a structured format that is known to us as the ABC of risk where:

A = Area
B = Boundaries/buildings
C = Contents

ESTABLISHING A SECURITY GRADE

To establish a security grade we should first carry out a simple pre-survey. This helps us to quickly gather information in our minds and to outline any perceived problems. In other words, just carry out a quick overview of the premises and its surroundings by walking around all those points to get a feel for the home and those areas of it that may not be particularly secure.

When we come to consider the premises we may wish to look at our house as comprising three essential points, i.e.

- 'the front'
- 'the back'
- 'the sides'

We say the front, the back and the sides because these three different essential points may all have their own features and vulnerabilities. For instance, the front of the house may be overlooked by other houses but the back of the house may back on to a wood or a secluded area. The side of the house could be an amalgamation of the two or have other considerations. Therefore, the risks to security can differ widely and this all needs to be taken into account in the final analysis.

Having gathered the information from the pre-survey in our minds, we can then set about preparing a full report to contain all of the required data. This report can include a small amount of floor plans or maps to help explain any areas of detail.

It is the case that we use the same ways of assessing the risks for all home types.

We need to produce a 'home risk assessment form' to contain all of the information.

When developing your form:

- Do be honest and critical.
- Don't exaggerate or over-inflate the information with maps or plans.

The first part of the form should give the home address, which should include the postcode of the property.

The second part should give information in respect of the home type/description. This need only be an overview because most of the information for the home will actually be included elsewhere in the form. So, an example for the home type/description we need only put:

Three-bedroom, semi-detached, two-storey home of brick construction with an attached garage.

The home has a medium-sized rear garden, which is bordered on all sides by other properties.

ABC of risk is the same for all building types. For every home risk assessment, no matter the building type or location, we use the ABC of risk. This is a method of compiling all of the required information in a recognized format.

A small open-aspect front garden with a single car drive is at the front of the home.

The full report, that we now need to complete, needs to use a descriptive chart to record the findings of the home risk assessment. It comprises three main sections, which are known as A, B and C, and cover the ABC of risk.

Consider Section A (*see* page 12)

To complete this section, first, we need to look at parts a–g and also look at the notes at the bottom of the section, as shown in the table.

We must then write in our findings for each part, i.e. a–g.

After that we need to make a decision as to what risk grade our findings warrant for each part where:

1 = low risk
2 = low to medium risk
3 = medium to high risk
4 = high risk

So, as an example for part a, we write in our findings as *Inner city – moderately high density* because that is the area population size. We then must decide on what we believe is a true risk grade from 1 to 4. Risk grade 3 has been decided in this example because it is inner city but only of moderately high density, and not of high density. All of the other parts of the section are then considered using a similar approach. It is convenient to use the risk grade numbers 1–4 because under the European Standards, security systems are ultimately graded as a risk grade from 1 to 4.

Consider Section B (*see* page 13)

Having completed Section A, we can then do the same for Section B, which covers buildings/boundaries. Once again look at the parts in this section, i.e. a–g, and also look at the notes at the end of the section. Then write in all of your assessment findings and risk grades for all of the parts a–g. As an example, parts a and b have been found to be generally secure;

GUIDE TO SECTION A RISK ASSESSMENT

Section A Findings/Area/Risk Grade

(a) Rural, suburban or inner city

Account for the density of population in which the home is situated, i.e. suburban has a medium density inhabitation
Inner city – moderately high density, risk grade 3.

(b) Area access to and from the premises

Ease of access to and from the premises to be established. Is access restricted?
Access is easy, risk grade 3.

(c) Local lighting in general area of premises

Establish if good levels of lighting are available in the local vicinity.
Very good lighting is available, risk grade 1.

(d) Similar home types in the area

Question if other houses are of the same type and architecture.
Many similar houses are in the area, risk grade 2.

(e) Previous intrusion and problem rates

Record any previous intrusion for the particular home and if the intrusion or problem rates for the neighbouring homes is of a low or high incidence level.
Very low incidence rates, risk grade 1.

(f) Rail and road infrastructure

Are there any advanced networks and intersections that can be used to gain access to and from the premises and then on to the rail and road links?
Yes the networks are advanced, risk grade 4.

(g) Vandalism history

Determine if vandalism for local area is higher than the surrounding areas.
Very low problem rate, risk grade 1.

Notes

The insurance industry sets its premiums in relation to the history of the area. The increasing density of the area reflects this.

Criminals prefer easy access to any premises that they target.

Superior lighting reduces the risk grade.

Particularly desirable homes of different architecture in the area to other more common types present an unwanted attraction to the criminal fraternity.

Previous intrusion rates reflect correspondingly high criminal activity in the area.

Advanced networks for road and rail links assist criminals to move between localities.

High vandalism rates suggest higher risk grades due to anti-social behaviour and unsociable neighbours.

GUIDE TO SECTION B RISK ASSESSMENT

Section B Findings/Buildings and Boundaries/Risk Grade

(a) Home type and construction

Make a record of the home type and its general construction and architecture.
Is the home multi- or single-storey and are there an unusually high number of entry points? Is the roof easily penetrated or any panels installed that would allow entry to the house?
Semi-detached brick building. Two floors. Secure construction, risk grade 2.

(b) Perimeter

Account for the good or poor repair, adequacy, and general construction and strength of the buildings and boundaries. Check if there are perimeter fences, any rivers adjacent to the buildings and if telephone lines on the perimeter of the building are vulnerable.
No particular vulnerable points. Boundaries generally are secure, risk grade 2.

(c) Lighting

Is the perimeter lit at night and is there lighting beyond the perimeter? Check if the lighting has protection against vandalism and what down-time for the lighting has been experienced in the past.
Very poor lighting overall, risk grade 4.
Level of risk X.

(d) Position and occupancy

Does shrubbery protect access to the building or does it have a reverse effect of obscuring the building? Do adjacent buildings provide any entry points? Consider if the building is of shared occupancy and if rooms within the building or apartment block facilitate a change of use.

(e) Physical attributes of structures

Height of home. Strength of doors, windows, walls, roof and frames. Check if there are vulnerable skylights, flat roofs and the security of locks and shutters.

(f) Scaling aids

Are there trees, strong drainpipes (particularly of old-style steel construction), scaffolding, drums or garden furniture that can be used or moved for climbing purposes? Are there any other climbing points or railings that could be used for scaling or are ladders or steps easily available?

(g) Boundary access

Are there any manned security schemes for the area or local CCTV schemes? Do any adjacent industries operate outside normal working hours?

Notes

The higher number of access points reflects in a relative increase in the number of security protection issues and systems required.

The perimeter is of vital importance as it forms the first line of security. Telephone lines may be needed to provide alarm signalling for security systems or to neighbours particularly for homes that may not be close to other houses.

Lighting is of high value for security at night but must have low down-times when in need of repair.

Occupancy of the building by others can compromise security and disclose local information to criminals.

Bungalows often offer many access points since they are of only one level. Flat roofs can provide access to vulnerable upper windows on houses.

Check for scaling aids that can be moved to vulnerable points.

Local security schemes reduce the security risk and are taken into account by the insurance industry.

GUIDE TO SECTION C RISK ASSESSMENT

Section C Findings/Contents/Risk Grade

(a) Transport

How can goods be carried away – lorry, car, people or other?

(b) Storage of possessions

Security of storage and storage area. Does the home have a safe? Is any storage of goods made in a vehicle that can be taken away from the home?

(c) Ease of transportation of goods

Consider the size/weight relationship. Check if valuables can be taken away by hand or in transportable containers.

(d) Contents' value

Record this in a log by room and also by total home area.

(e) Specific value goods

Are there any specific high-value goods that may be kept in the home and could knowledge of these be available to the criminal fraternity.

Notes

The easy transportation of goods from the scene increases the risk grade.

Safe boxes and the employment of concealed points decrease the risk grade.

Size and weight relationship is important as small, light high-value goods are high risk.

Detail rooms of significance individually in the assessment.

Pay particular attention to any special goods.

---

therefore, their overall risk grades have been given as *risk grade 2.*

Consider Section C (*see* above)

Having completed Section B we can then do the same for Section C, which covers contents. Once again, look at the parts in this section, i.e. a–e, and also look at the notes at the end of the section. Then write in all of your assessment findings and risk grades for all of the parts a–e.

People

When the ABC of risk has been determined, we need to decide if any people associated with the home can influence the risk assessment. For instance, there may be staff employed in the larger home or, for any premises, there may be cleaners, cooks, and so on. Assessing people is complex but we need to make any notes in regard to staff history, turnover, vetting, roles, breeches of confidentiality and access to valuables.

For the smaller home we may need to take account of the influence of children or older persons who may live there or visit regularly.

Additional Information

All that then remains is the introduction of a final section to include any additional information for more diverse issues such as the presence of dogs or wardens visiting the home. There may also be storage of valuable items that need to be considered and contact numbers for key-holders or security maintenance personnel.

THE HOME RISK ASSESSMENT FORM

Having recorded all of the information for Sections A, B and C, and then considered the People and any Additional Information assessment areas, we are now able to produce the final home risk assessment form. In it, we may want to include certain special risk level information at the end of the form or make particular notes about special risks.

Remember that everyone will produce a form to suit their own preferences in terms of its layout and the amount of information they feel necessary. However, it needs to include information for the three sections A, B and C, plus any other essential information.

Some people may also want to include a few floor plans or maps but these should not be too detailed or elaborate.

Once the home risk assessment form has been almost completed, it is possible we may want to identify some areas of concern in terms of special risks posed.

DETERMINING SPECIAL RISK LEVELS

If we want to add a special priority to any particular issue identified in the home risk

---

Home Risk Assessment

Home address ....

....

Home type/description ....

....

Section A   Area ....

....

Section B   Buildings/boundaries ....

....

Section C   Contents ....

....

People ....

....

Additional information ....

....

Special risks level ....

....

Home risk assessment form. The completed home risk assessment form should contain an overview of the home and a description of it, the written assessment findings and risk grades for the three Sections A, B and C. It may also contain any issues with regard to people plus any other particular additional information and details of special risks levels.

---

assessment form, we can take a level of risk and then apply it to that part. This helps us to determine and then identify the risk levels. However, we only need to do this for any special part that we think needs attention. For instance, we could apply level of risk X to part c of Section B in order to reflect the priority of it being an urgent risk to security and needing attention as soon as possible (see table overleaf).

GUIDE TO SPECIAL RISK LEVELS

Level of risk	Priority	Action
XX	Unacceptable risk to security	Immediate remedial action is needed
X	Urgent risk to security	Needs attention as soon as possible to remove risk
Y1	Priority	Establish if risk can be reduced and a satisfactory procedure put in place
Y2	Low priority	Needs attention within near future
Y	Very low priority	Needs attention when possible

It remains to say that the home risk assessment must use standard procedures and follow a recognized sequence of events, taking into account all of the measures mentioned if the risks are to be identified and properly documented.

Of course we need a thoughtful home security approach when we perform the assessment, so keep an open mind and think of how we need to:

- Fight complacency.
- Deal with apathy.
- Take stock of what is important to us.
- Come to accept any unpleasant realities we may find.

Once the assessment has all been completed it becomes possible for us to look into the requirements the insurance industry will impose and the ways in which we can improve our overall security.

Rather interesting is the fact that we will use, and hear, many expressions related to security, such as low security, medium security and high security. We also naturally use the same terms related to risk and levels, or we may hear expressions of minimum security and maximum security. These are all generic terms and none can be defined in a specific way. By using these terms, it at least indicates the general level of risk that must apply to the home, even though interpretation of the scale will differ in the eyes of different people.

Taking the bottom or minimum scale, I suppose we could say that security must at least impede some unauthorized external activity, so has to employ simple physical barriers and regular locks with some essential electronic security system. Going on a stage to the middle of the scale, we need improved physical barriers and upgraded locking with a relative improvement in our electronic security systems supported by maintenance contracts. Of course, at the high end of the scale we need to involve specialists for the different disciplines. This is needed to achieve the most effective solution based on a balanced judgement with back-up services and contingency plans.

The important thing is to have all the findings from the risk assessment clearly identified in writing on the form in such a way that it is easy to follow and can be checked or overviewed by another party for any level on the security scale; this ensures that there can be no confusion. We can move on to take the necessary measures found as a result of having carried out the home risk assessment.

However, there are a number of special considerations that have an effect on how we implement our home security. It is these things that we need to look at next.

THE IMPLEMENTATION OF HOME SECURITY

There are certain issues that we face when implementing our home security. These differ depending upon how involved or complex the work will be. Some may be administrative procedures or dealing with regulatory authorities and the insurance companies. Others involve organizing the addition of physical security devices and electronic systems. For certain tasks we may be able to do the work ourselves, but for others we need to seek the help of professionals. So in these instances involving practical elements there are questions we need to ask ourselves.

We are now about to have a look at how we need to ensure that we do not pass on information that may create security problems. We also need to give some thought as to how we must retain information responsibly. But before going on to these stages, let us first recap on the important features and attributes of the home risk assessment (see diagram overleaf).

Disclosure of Information

We have noted that we need to consider people in our risk assessment. It is also the case that we may have to involve others in the implementation of our practical security measures. However, it is clear that we do not want to disclose information to persons who could then pass on, or use, any information that compromises our security. This information could be obtained and passed on in a number of ways. It can be by visitors to the house, persons carrying out work for us or through an electronic means such as criminals viewing

---

GUIDE TO THE IMPLEMENTATION OF PRACTICAL SECURITY MEASURES IN RESIDENTIAL HOMES

Installation of Physical Security – General
- For any work carried out on the perimeter or fabric of the home, including building work, we need to ensure that it meets local authority requirements.
- If we use outside contractors for our own protection, we need confirmation that the work will be to relevant standards and the contractor is accountable to a trade association or regulatory body.
- We can always ask for references from past customers.
- We also need to ask if we will receive written specifications and a copy of terms and conditions for the work.

Installation of Electronic Security and Lighting Systems – General
- The installation of any electronic or electrical system will, to some extent, involve wiring either in or around the home, which is governed by the Wiring Regulations.
- Make checks to confirm that the installer is competent to carry out the work and if an approved installer is required. This will ensure that any work will meet the needs of the insurance company underwriting the home policy.
- Check to see if a 24-hour contact line is available and if there is any maintenance contract.
- Confirm if the equipment is outright purchase or lease.

Notes
In all cases find out how much the work will cost and check for ongoing charges such as maintenance contracts.
Never assume there will be no disruption to the home for practical services carried out – check what the disruption could be.

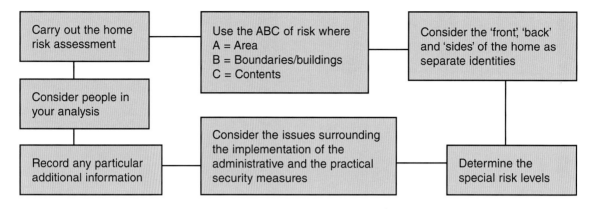

Architecture. Home risk assessment.

our internet activities to obtain personal information. The subject of organized crime is a serious one, alongside identity theft.

So we need to guard sensitive information that has an influence on our home security.

It is important that we must destroy any personal information papers and documents, including utility bills, that are no longer needed and never put these items casually in bins that could be accessed by criminals. Shredding machines are available to shred such documents so that the information held on them is no longer accessible.

Telephone Security

When we consider the disclosure of information, we have to think beyond ourselves because there are two family groups that can be tricked more easily into giving away information. These are namely children and senior citizens. We need to ensure that we offer the support to ensure these vulnerable people cannot be put into a position where they can be pumped for information. It could even be the case that they offer information against our knowledge. The most likely way is through telephone calls to the home. We ourselves need to be alert to callers who claim to be representing official businesses but try to obtain personal information for a different

purpose. It is surprising the number of people who are prepared to take a telephone call and speak to the caller without any certainty as to who the caller actually is.

To retain information that is important to us it is obvious we need to know with certainty the identity of the caller and even then we should never divulge anything that could in any way compromise our security.

In terms of children and senior citizens we can only add that these groups should be instructed to talk on the telephone only to persons they know, otherwise the caller should call back later. A legitimate caller will not object to such a request.

Postal Devices

The final thing we may wish to consider is anything delivered to us through the mail. We need to have a policy to deal with all mail or any packages received at the home and in particular with those that claim to contain information. This policy is to be followed by all of the home users.

These devices can pose a threat to us. So if we suspect having received a package or letter that could pose a danger *do not open it* until it has been inspected.

Be aware of packages marked with restrictive instructions such as:

GUIDE TO DISCLOSURE OF INFORMATION ISSUES IN RESIDENTIAL HOMES

Visitors to the House

- Be aware of cold callers who offer services or may claim to be carrying out research.
- These people may be looking for an excuse to get close to the house to obtain information.
- If quotes are obtained for work and sales people are to be allowed in the house, only provide information specific to the needs of the project.
- Do not give information as to when the house may or may not be occupied.
- Ensure that visitors to the house are unable to see confidential mail. Make sure that mail cannot be collected by unauthorized people.
- Lockable mail boxes are available for those instances where mail is delivered to the perimeter of the home, such as at the end of a driveway.

Persons Carrying Out Work

- Ensure these persons are traceable.
- Unless these persons are known to you, use reputable trade-approved companies that have vetting practices for their staff.
- Remember that the representative who does the survey will probably not be the person who carries out the work. Be aware that a number of persons may be involved in the project, all of whom could then have access to information regarding the house.

Disposal of Documents

- Ensure that documents holding personal information or utility bills are destroyed.
- Do not dispose of such papers or documents with the household waste as they could be accessed by criminals.

Internet Security

- If using the internet, security software is essential to ensure that your data and personal information are protected. Antivirus software scans the PC or laptop and removes any viruses and spyware. Internet security software also has a firewall to block attacks via the internet and protect against phishing sites. Always install updates.
- Criminals will try to obtain personal data and also information for your house and may pass details on to others.

- Personal
- Private and confidential
- Do not X-ray
- Open this end only
- Do not delay – open now

Also be aware of:

- Mail or packages with no return address.
- Unexpected items.
- Items marked with threatening language.
- Inappropriate or unusual labelling.

- Excessive packaging material, such as tape or string.
- Not addressed to a specific person.
- Excessive postage with too many stamps.
- Poorly typed or distorted handwriting.

If a suspect mail or package is received, place it in a plastic bag or container in case it includes a chemical, and have it inspected thoroughly.

We can now go forward a stage to look at the requirements of the insurance industry and burglary prevention, which are covered in the next chapter.

chapter two

Insurance Requirements and Burglary Prevention

In this chapter we are going to have a look at the requirements of the insurance companies in terms of their policies and how they assign their elements of risk and premiums. The next step is to overview the fundamentals of household burglary prevention. From that we will turn our attention specifically to gardens, garages and outbuildings, as these are often the first target for the intruder. Then we will investigate the subject of bogus callers and include guidance on how to avoid becoming a victim of distraction and artifice burglary. We will also touch on sneak thieves, vandalism and trespassers.

To most of us, home insurance is a grudge purchase because we see ourselves buying something that we really never want to have to use. Or in other words, we buy something in the hope it is never needed. However, we may also believe that if the worst comes to the worst, the insurance policy will at least cover the loss suffered … but will it? Well, with any insurance policy there will inevitably be a list of requirements and exclusions that apply before the insurance company will pay out on a claim. Therefore, policies should always be read in detail, as any summary of the policy may not give all the information needed. In addition, the insurance company is entitled to expect the policy holder to take care to avoid the events that the policy actually covers.

This all means that we should not rely on insurance alone to cover us for any loss because in the real world we always need to take precautions of our own to avoid any such loss. Not just that but we want to avoid being the victims of crime in any event, hence the reason for making sure that we have satisfactory security in place for ourselves and our home.

INSURANCE REQUIREMENTS

Most contents policies have similar terms regarding minimum security requirements for general risks. This is all influenced by the Association of British Insurers (ABI) who are the voice of the UK's insurance, investment and long-term savings industry. Typically these requirements and conditions of the policy may include or involve all of the following:

- The use of a five-lever mortise deadlock, automatic rim deadlock or integral multi-point locking system on the front door. All other external doors should have the same level of security. As an alternative, they could be fitted with key-operated bolts.
- Garages and outbuildings capable of being locked with a key.
- Downstairs windows and other windows that are accessible should be lockable with a key.
- All doors and windows are to be locked when the house is unoccupied or at night.

(This may not apply in the policy to windows in an occupied bedroom.)

- The property should not be unoccupied for longer than a period specified in the policy – this could be as little as thirty days.
- Any theft or (criminal) damage must immediately be reported to the police and a report number issued.
- Insurance policies usually also contain a list of exclusions, i.e. types of loss and also damage that are not covered. These tend to include theft by someone the householder has let into the property or theft if the property is left unoccupied for an extended period.
- High-value or some special goods may have to be insured individually in their own right. They may need a particular security system installed to offer protection to them.
- The insurance premium may be reduced if security systems, such as intruder alarms, are installed and maintained.
- When agreeing to provide cover, insurance companies rely on information provided by the applicant. Often this information will be provided verbally and it may not be backed up by any documentary evidence.

The information provided determines the terms of the policy and the premium payable. A person applying for insurance has a legal duty to give accurate information in 'the utmost good faith'. If the information provided is misleading, incomplete or wrong, the policy on which it is based will almost certainly be invalid. Changes of circumstances that may affect the validity of a policy include a member of the household working from home, a member of the household being convicted of an offence or a lodger moving in.

To maximize the chances that a policy will pay out, policy holders must ensure that they give the correct information to the insurance company and that they inform the insurance company if there is a change in circumstances.

On the basis of the foregoing, it is clear that we have insurance only for the loss that could be suffered, whereas in real terms we do not want to have to suffer the loss in the first place.

If a loss occurs as a result of burglary, we do not just suffer from the consequences of the burglary alone but also have to deal with all of the claims processes and associated administrative procedures. We may also lose as a consequence of our premiums being increased.

Always expect the unexpected and never think that accidents only happen to other people because someday we may become those other people.

The elements of risk that our security details are assigned to avoid and eliminate need to be kept up to date. If we maintain and control our direction and objectives, then our risk factor can be reduced substantially.

So with those thoughts on what insurance is actually geared towards, we can now overview the logic of household burglary prevention and its foundations.

HOUSEHOLD BURGLARY PREVENTION

Before we look at burglary prevention we need to appreciate the 'theft triangle'. According to this concept three elements are present, namely motive, desire and opportunity.

- **Motive.** This is the reason to steal.
- **Desire.** This is an extension on the motive, as it presents distinct rewards for the criminal.
- **Opportunity.** This is the chance that the criminal has and relates very much to the absence of the barriers that are presented

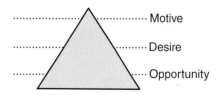

Theft triangle. The homeowner can only control the 'Opportunity' element within the theft triangle in order to improve their security.

to them to stop home burglary. It is this that is the responsibility of the security we implement, because the motive and desire are beyond the scope of our security policies and practices.

When we come to look at household burglary prevention measures, give some thought to the cumulative effect. In other words do not think of one element in isolation being what we need to satisfy our security issues. Think more of a range of corrective elements that can be used to give us overall security. If we see our security being the accumulation of many factors added together to protect us against a diverse range of problems, then we will be better served.

Do not attempt to only look at one facet and fail to look at all of the other security threats that confront us. It is the effect of a number of things together that we must use to protect ourselves, our family and our possessions.

Also, when you come to consider your burglary prevention measures try to put yourself in the place of the burglar and think like a burglar!

We have come to accept that the use of physical force as a means of defence of property by a homeowner is a possible justification used by defendants who argue that they should not be held liable for the loss they may have caused when defending their property. Courts have generally agreed that the use of force by a homeowner may be acceptable. Therefore, a person may use such force as is reasonable in the circumstances in the prevention of crime or in arresting offenders or suspects.

So, in so far as an attack on a property is a crime, reasonable force may be used to prevent the crime or to arrest the offender, whether it is related to the theft of a sum of money or the damage of an object.

In many cases of robbery and burglary the threat will be to both the person and the property. However, we do not want to get into a situation where we need to use force to deal with a burglar, so we initially need to seek out the ways to stop this situation developing in the first place. But we have a problem trying to say specifically how we can implement burglary prevention because there are so many ways in which burglary can be committed. It can be done by breaking into the home by using a variety of methods or it can be by bogus calling. Therefore, we have to study burglary prevention as a part of our wider security issues.

A person is said to be guilty of burglary if they enter any building or part of a building as a trespasser and steal or have an intention to steal, inflict grievous bodily harm or to do unlawful damage to the building or anything in it.

Let us start by looking at a few of the fundamentals associated with burglary:

- Burglars like to 'graduate'. They become confident if successful by stealing from 'soft targets' first, before moving on to tackle more difficult profitable targets.
- If they are successful with committing burglary at a particular target, they often return to it or tackle a similar target or area. Having gained a learning curve for a particular home or area, they will want to use it or pass on information to other criminals.
- They are worried about being trapped in a house or disturbed. For this reason they will start by tackling such 'soft targets' as gardens, garages and outbuildings that are detached from the main residence. If seen or disturbed they have a far greater opportunity to run from the scene, so cannot be trapped easily.
- Burglars prefer to break in through doors rather than through windows. Once in a home or building they will then try to ensure that an external door or doors are open so they can run from the scene if confronted. They will not want to exit through a window or take goods through it. For this reason patio doors/French doors, and suchlike, are often attacked first or are forced open

immediately after the home has been broken into.

- All homes are potential targets. Hardened criminals are prepared to target almost any home.

In order to anticipate the risk of crime we must therefore:

- Identify the main crime targets.
- Assess how we intend to provide the level of protection required.
- Examine the facilities that we already have.

From this we will then be able to go on to implement our security measures and strategies. Remember that we may wish to consider our house of being formed from three essential areas or typically the front, the back and the sides.

Remember every burglar naturally prefers soft targets.

It is interesting that a high percentage of burglars, when interviewed, indicated that they prefer to visit a potential target many times in advance of attacking the premises. This is to gain information and to check to see if any security measures are in place and if it is going to be a difficult target.

Although many burglars act on opportunity, this is certainly not always the case. So, if not all criminals only act on opportunity, we need to believe that we could always be under surveillance from would-be burglars.

Sadly some people can be targeted many times as the burglar may become confident, believe the homeowner may have recovered any previously stolen goods following an insurance payout and hence decide to attack the home once again. In other words, the burglar may feel confident and return to the house once more or even a number of times more in the belief that they can achieve the same results over and over again.

So from this, and accepting the philosophy that burglars do like to start with targets such as

gardens, garages and outbuildings, let us look at these in a little detail.

GARDENS, GARAGES AND OUTBUILDINGS

Householders should check their household insurance policies to see if they cover theft from the garden, garage or from any outbuildings on their land. These areas may not be covered by the standard home policy, since they can be subject to special risks.

The homeowner must take care to prevent intruders from getting access to their land and ultimately to gardens, garages and sheds, as they may contain a number of high-value items, such as lawnmowers, bicycles and even garden furniture.

These areas may also contain items like tools and ladders, which a burglar can use to break into the house. Therefore the criminal would not need to transport tools or climbing aids to the scene that is being targeted.

We should first assess the outskirts of the home, as a secure perimeter will always help to deter thieves who may initially enter the outskirts of the home with a view to targeting the garden, garage or outbuildings.

GUIDE TO A SECURE PERIMETER

Check the Perimeter

- Check the walls, gates, fences and hedges bordering the property. Identify any weak spots that could provide easy access to intruders or vehicles, and secure where necessary.
- Consider restricting access at your entrance. This prevents unwelcome vehicles entering. Ensure that gates are robust and cannot be removed.
- Install security lighting around the perimeter. This is to include all of the borders of the home and garden. (We deal with options for this in Chapter 5).

Next we can consider the buildings.

GUIDE TO SECURE BUILDINGS

The Buildings

- Fit windows with metal bars or grilles.
- Fit high-security mortise padlocks on doors.
- Ensure doors and windows are well maintained and in a good state of repair.
- Give some thought to installing a steel external door or with a steel panel.
- Do not overlook the possibility that criminals may attempt to gain access through the roof of the building
- Replace ordinary screws on outbuilding doors with non-return screws.
- Obscure the windows of your shed/garage to prevent thieves from seeing what you have inside.
- If valuable items must be stored in garages or outbuildings, install a metal cage to contain these goods.
- Garage defenders are available to protect all doors and are particularly effective with 'up and over' doors. These are very secure and can be supplemented with vehicle posts that are removable if needs demand.
- Allied to the garage defender a car-parking post that can be pushed down, or leant over when not in use, can be used to stop a car from being moved from its parked position. These can be fitted adjacent to the garage building for additional vehicle use.
- Use strong hasps to secure garden sheds.

GUIDE TO SECURING THE CONTENTS

The Contents

- Ensure that ladders and climbing aids such as steps and tools are particularly well-secured.
- Mark all removable items such as bicycles, lawnmowers, hedge trimmers and garden furniture with your postcode and house number.
- Keep a list of tools together with serial numbers and any identification marks.
- Shackle large items such as bicycles and lawnmowers together and, if possible, secure to a permanent fixture such as a cemented metal post.
- Attach ladders and spades to a secure fixture.
- Use an ultra-violet marking system on goods.

Although wherever possible we should avoid storing valuable goods in garages and outbuildings, there are extra precautions for securing the contents.

It is worth remembering that good physical restraints, such as grilles, panels and bars, in conjunction with strong doors and windows help to protect our goods because a burglar needs tools of some description to overcome these restraints. Therefore, a potential burglar must come equipped with tools or use some that are already at the scene.

The main plus, or things in our favour, in terms of fitting security aids to garages, outbuildings and sheds, is that it is easier than installing them around the home. This is because we do not have the problems with aesthetics or decorative problems, so we are able to carry out the tasks with less hindrance.

We do, however, have a problem with garages, outbuildings and sheds if the weakest part of the perimeter of them is eventually breached and, of course, the physical perimeter can only ever be as strong as the weakest part.

The problem we have is that once the burglar has entered the building they then have time to try to select goods as the criminal is no longer visible to the homeowner or any passer-by. For this reason it is always worth supplementing our physical security measures with electronic security systems, as these systems have volumetric protection, i.e. they protect the inner spaces of the outbuildings. This volumetric protection stops the intruder from spending time in the outbuildings because it generates an alarm condition when it senses human presence. The extent to which we do this should be governed by how high we place the risk of intrusion.

So we can use a purpose-installed alarm system for the outbuildings or, if we have an intruder alarm system installed in the home, it is always possible to extend this to the outbuildings. This can be done by running alarm cables between the outbuildings and home or, if this is difficult, it can be carried out by a wireless radio technique, so no cables need to be involved.

Furthermore there are particular electronic systems known to us as perimeter intruder detection systems (PIDS) that are widely used to protect the outside areas, whilst the internal building areas can benefit from the installation of intruder alarms to some extent or other.

Let us look at PIDS next.

Perimeter Intruder Detection Systems (PIDS)

It is a challenging experience to select outside electronic security systems protection because the areas to be protected are not as easily defined as the internal rooms or areas of the home or its outbuildings.

For high-risk areas, specialist detection systems are available. Sensors can be attached to posts or fences or they can be buried under the ground to form detection zones. These detect attempts to climb over fences or they recognize disturbance of the ground as it is walked on or as vehicles pass over them. All of these systems are effective at detecting intruders at the outskirts of the premises and preventing intrusion. They are a progression on electrified fences which are now only used for high-risk commercial risks.

An audible alarm or voice warning system can be generated locally to deter the intruder with any PIDS system. The former is used to draw attention to the area and the latter is an announcement that notifies an intruder that they have been detected and they are to leave the area immediately.

Alternatively, remote signalling can be made to a control point or CCTV cameras may be activated so the actual events at the scene can be viewed and recorded for evidential purposes.

For the more general risks associated with outside areas for homes, beam detection systems are an excellent proposition. Although there are a number of technologies available to us, including microwave detection, the most

popular forms are infra-red based. Two versions of detection devices are available; they are known to us as passive infra-red (PIR) and active infra-red (IR).

Passive Infra-Red (PIR)

These detection devices represent excellent value for money. They are weatherproof when used for outside applications and are ideal to protect a clearly defined space, such as the area around a vulnerable patio. PIRs are used with many lighting systems to bring on lighting when they sense a person or vehicle entering a particular outside area. They are known as movement detectors and have a wide range of protection patterns that can be selected to suit the installation and only need mounting so they are not easily attacked by criminals.

In practice they can also bring on sounders (or any other warning or signalling devices), but are not generally used to do so, as they are affected by changing ambient temperatures and pulsating heat sources in the areas they view, leading to occasional false alarms or sporadic activation. Audible signalling could hence be an irritation to neighbouring properties. However, for mainstream and medium-risk security, and the detection of persons or vehicles with a view to energizing lighting, they are an excellent proposition as the occasional false activation is not a real handicap when balanced against their highly cost-efficient service. Therefore they are used in extremely high volume in the domestic market for the wide-scale protection of homes.

PIR/microwave dual technology versions, with an increased resistance to false activations, are available to the professional security systems installation industry for their customized or specialist installations.

Active Infra-Red (IR)

These adopt what is known as a 'beam-break' technique. They operate using an active transmitter and receiver that are mounted a certain distance apart. This distance can be in the order of 100m. An invisible beam is sent between the transmitter and receiver, which, if broken by a person or vehicle passing through the beam, generates an alarm condition.

These active devices have techniques that make them virtually false-alarm free, so they are ideal to protect open drive entrance areas and the areas running parallel with fences.

The transmitters and receivers are capable of being blended into the environment or the architecture of their surroundings so they are not easily seen by an observer. IRs are a particularly good proposition for the outside of the home for generating an alarm signal. However, they are a more expensive option than the PIR in terms of purchase and installation costs.

All of these PIDS are clearly a progression on old-style generation devices, such as trip wires, which, as their name suggests, were wires that were run around an outside area of the home. If these wires were disturbed by an intruder, who may touch them, an alarm was caused to sound.

So it follows that for our gardens, garage and outbuildings we have many electronic detection system options that are available to us. These are all capable of being linked to lighting or other signalling options, such as sounders or buzzers, or they may activate cameras for viewing purposes. Alternatively they may activate voice warning systems to relay a pre-recorded warning message to intruders.

In the first instance though we always need to arrange our physical restraints and then supplement them, as necessary, with external outside electronic security systems protection. We may also add internal protection by fitting such basic deterrents as DIY shed alarms that protect the interior of the buildings and give audible warnings of an intrusion.

If we also shackle valuables, this stops an intruder grabbing goods and trying to run from the scene with the alarm sounding. The intruder will not be keen on trying to unshackle goods in the building with an alarm sounding, although they will always be prepared to grab any loose items as they flee, especially if this does not hinder the speed of their escape.

As an extension on this we may extend the house alarm to the outbuildings and shed, etc., by using radio transmitters and receivers, or we may install a designated intruder alarm security system in these buildings and then link it to the house either by wiring or by the transmitter/receiver method. Either technique allows the shed and outbuildings security system to be integrated with that of the home.

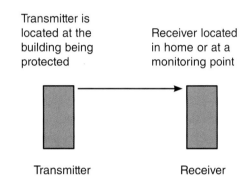

Transmitter is located at the building being protected

Receiver located in home or at a monitoring point

Transmitter   Receiver

Signal is sent between transmitter and receiver by wireless radio signal.
This is a useful method of linking systems or buildings, particularly when it is difficult to install wires or cables.

Transmitter/receiver link method.

We are now able to overview the architecture of how we approach our burglary protection methods in relation to our garden, garage and outbuildings (see page 27).

Let us move on now and look at a completely different type of burglary prevention and how to deal with bogus callers. However, before we do this it is interesting to note that during a burglary the criminal will be stressed so has adrenalin pumping quickly through their body. This adrenalin is there as a natural process to increase the potential energy of the body so if that person is confronted or attacked their body can respond in the same way as an animal

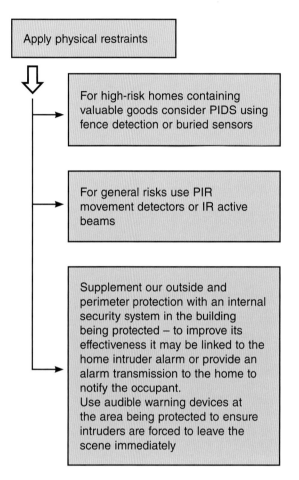

Architecture of burglary protection methods in relation to our garden, garage and outbuildings.

intruder, the criminals response can be very unpredictable. Burglars are always reluctant to target bungalows during the night when the occupants are at home asleep because they are on the same level of the building and can be confronted easier and quicker if the homeowner awakens. For this reason an intruder will be more prepared to target a two-storey house during the night when the occupants are asleep upstairs.

It all goes to say we have to avoid the associated problems of intrusion in the first place by instigating burglary prevention measures.

So let us gather our thoughts and, for guidance purposes, summarize the basics:

- We need to understand the role and minimum security requirements of the insurance companies.
- We need to know that burglars tend to start with soft targets, such as gardens, garages and outbuildings, and then graduate.
- We must consider the perimeter, building and contents as three separate subjects.
- We need to apply our physical restraints and then supplement this with our electronic security, whilst giving some thought to the use of sounders, lighting, CCTV, voice warning systems and so on.
- We must employ security measures to avoid confrontation with intruders and possible personal injury.

Bogus callers and sneak thieves represent a rather different threat or risk to our home security.

BOGUS CALLERS

The home risk assessment helps us to identify the risks that are associated with an individual or the property to be protected so we can put into effect measures to reduce the risks that are presented to us. As an extension on this subject we must be alert to those who may

in the wild – it can either run or it can stand and fight. Normally the burglar will run, but not always.

We often hear people say an intruder must have been disturbed because that criminal left the scene quickly without taking everything they had selected. In reality it is more likely the intruder responded to a slight noise, such as a floorboard creaking, by suddenly panicking and then running off as they would be in a highly charged physiological state. This state makes the homeowner vulnerable because if they do happen to return home or disturb an not attempt to break into homes but will try to trick or con their way in. These people are known as bogus callers pretending to be on official business from respectable concerns, or they may pretend to be tradesmen or workmen calling to carry out urgent repair work.

Over the years we have also referred to these people as con artists or con men because they enter the confidence of the victim by using a kind approach or they use deceit. Unfortunately these people can be found resorting to a variety of different means to gain access to homes but the end result is always the same, in that they intend to steal or they may try to overcharge for services. These offenders may succeed because they sound believable, so we must not be fooled. It is important to make sure that they are who they claim to be.

To protect ourselves from bogus callers we must take certain precautions. With regard to the installation of security aids, it is wise to have a door chain installed and also a door viewer at the area that a caller would attend such as the front door.

It is possible to supplement the door chain and viewer with a personal attack (PA) button adjacent to the door at the point where the caller would attend the house. This could be connected to a security system intruder alarm. If an unwelcome caller was to visit the house and become abusive or threatening, the homeowner would be able to push the button causing the alarm to immediately activate and bring attention to the house, forcing the unwelcome caller to leave the premises. In fact a variety of PAs are available to do this, including versions with timers. To operate these timer types, the user pushes a button, which starts a preset timer. The caller is then told that if they do not leave within a set time, the alarm will automatically activate. If the caller leaves willingly, the user simply cancels the timer.

It is the case that in advance of making a call the bogus caller may spend some time viewing the house in order to find out how many persons are normally at home and the age groups of the occupants. They may then select a particular

time of the day or week to attend the premises, so they do not always act on opportunism. This should be given consideration if any particularly vulnerable person is always in the house at the same time of the day or to a given time schedule because the bogus caller may be selective as to when to call.

Remember that anyone can be a victim of clever bogus callers. Sadly some groups are targeted more than others, so many victims share certain characteristics. For instance many older women living alone are very trusting of others, even strangers. Loneliness, willingness to help and a sense of charity are examples of characteristics a bogus caller may exploit to enter a person's confidence.

These con people may also survive because their victims became embarrassed or the victim simply, for a variety of reasons, just does not want to go to the extent of reporting and giving details of an uncomfortable event.

We have two types of burglary to consider. These are namely distraction burglary and artifice burglary, although there can be an overlap of circumstances and outcomes between them.

DISTRACTION AND ARTIFICE BURGLARY

Distraction Burglary

First of all let us consider the crime-prevention methods that help us to avoid distraction burglary:

- Check the identity of the caller by calling the company they are reporting to be from, i.e. gas, electricity, water, police, and so on. Use the telephone numbers listed in your local directory or provided independently by your service provider – do not use any telephone numbers provided by the caller – they may be bogus.
- Don't keep large quantities of cash at home; put it in the bank where it is safe.

- Keep doors locked and windows secure at all times.
- Ensure that if you do let somebody in to your home, you close the door behind them – distraction burglars often work in teams, where one will distract you whilst others sneak in through the insecure door.
- If somebody asks for your help – needs to make a telephone call, lost a ball in your garden, needs a drink or pen and paper, for example, refer them to a younger neighbour or assist them through a closed door. Alternatively, call a friend or neighbour to come and assist.
- If you are not convinced of the identity of the caller, don't let them in. Ask the caller to come back later and arrange for a friend, relative or neighbour to be present on their return, or ask the caller to contact this person.
- Treat every stranger with caution. If you are still worried, dial 999 immediately and ask for the police.

Artifice Burglary

Artifice burglary may also be called trickery burglary and is a further method used by bogus callers.

These callers seem to concentrate on the homes of older people; for example, sheltered housing and housing estates designed for older people, which may be identified by ramps and hand rails by the front door. They often disguise themselves by dressing smartly and claiming to be from the council, police, health, gas, water or the electricity company.

Bogus callers can be convincing and persuasive, and may occasionally use children under the pretext that they need to retrieve their ball from the garden, use the toilet or have a drink of water. They can also turn up as builders or gardeners and try to trick the homeowner into paying for unnecessary work.

It is important not to pay in advance and to decline any offer to drive the homeowner to the bank to withdraw money. These are all excuses to gain admittance.

Handbags or wallets should not be left unattended in any room where a caller may need to enter. It is also important to stay with a caller and keep all other doors closed. People often keep their money in the dressing table, wardrobe, spare handbag or sideboard drawer – all places a bogus caller is likely to check.

A note of all reference numbers and phone numbers can be kept by the front door to make checking easier. Cards for this purpose may be available from your local Age Concern, home beat police officer, or neighbourhood watch co-ordinator.

It is important also to not purchase anything from a salesperson at the door – this includes furniture and valuables or any other possessions.

Of course there are growing concerns in protecting our senior citizens. We are finding increasing numbers of the senior citizen population and life expectancies are increasing according to most health organizations. Many seniors are living and surviving Alzheimer's disease and other dementias. Many are cared for by an ageing spouse or are alone without residential care-providers. In addition, some criminals change their victim of choice to the senior citizen so as to focus on those who have wealth or are more susceptible to a ruse. Many seniors may indeed not have a great technical affinity with a bank so may keep given amounts of cash in the house. Coupled with this may be loneliness or the want for a casual conversation that can set them up to become a victim.

So, in order to protect our senior citizens, have a policy, and try to get the message through to such groups, of the practices of what they are to do when callers come to the home.

The important thing to remember is that the official caller will never be irritated by the checks that any concerned homeowner decides to make (see box overleaf).

So remember that in all cases, there is never any problem in applying the time-honoured philosophy – if in doubt keep them out!

GOOD PRACTICE – CHECKLIST OF WHAT TO DO

When answering the door remember:

- To put the chain on.
- To check the identity of the caller by using the door viewer or, if you find moving about difficult, you could look through a window.
- To check the identity of the caller by calling the company they are reporting to be from.
- If you are not sure about the identity of the caller, call through the door or an adjacent window and ask the caller to say who he or she is and why they are calling; or open the door, still keeping the chain on, and inspect the caller's pass.
- All callers from the water, gas, or electricity company or local authority, who may need to enter your home, should have a pass to identify themselves. Gas, electricity and water companies are all required to offer special services for their customers of pensionable age. One of the services is to arrange for you to have a personal password so that you will know if the caller is a representative of the company. To register for these services you will need to contact the company. Information on how to do this is on the back of your bill.
- If you are not completely satisfied that the caller is who they say they are, ask for some other form of identification, such as your customer reference number – these can be found on the respective bills from the companies.

The police terminology for bogus callers is artifice burglary; and to enter as a trespasser and steal, artifice trickery. However, most people would still like to use the historic term con man or woman.
Remember also that bogus callers will:

- Call unannounced.
- Usually work in pairs.
- They will not generally have any type of uniform or arrive in any official van.
- They will not be willing for you to study their identity (if they have any).
- They will try and make you feel under pressure.
- If they gain entry into your home, one will stay with you whilst the other one will go to another part of the house.
- If they are working alone, then they will ask you to do something that separates you from them.

Official callers will:

- Try and make an appointment where possible. They will have your personal details on record and will be able to write/phone for an appointment.
- Will only be too happy for you to look at the ID they carry.
- Will usually wear a corporate rate uniform, and may have an official van.
- Will understand if you do not let them in, and should not put you under pressure.
- If in the house, will only go to one point, e.g. the gas or electric meter, kitchen stopcock.
- Will want you to stay with them.

Remember also to join any neighbourhood watch scheme for your area because of the benefits it brings. Police departments always function better with the assistance of responsible citizens.

Some people may not call the police because they are not exactly aware of what seemingly innocent activities might be and are hesitant to call for fear of being called a nosy neighbour.

Others take it for granted that someone else has called the police. In reality anything that seems a little 'out of place' for the area or time of day at which it occurs may mean criminal activity.

Some important things to watch for include persons loitering, peering into parked cars or taking an interest in the layout and amount of pedestrian traffic in the neighbourhood.

Checking the ID of a caller. Official callers will always carry professional ID and not be concerned if you want to check their credentials. In order to ensure that they are acting on professional business, the caller should be retained at a secure and external point when you make your telephone call.

For sure, not every stranger who comes into a neighbourhood is a criminal by any means. However, criminals may take the guise of legitimate persons. I suppose it is fair to say that if every criminal looked like a criminal then they would be spotted immediately. So watchers can reduce crime but it is ideal if neighbourhood watch schemes can be introduced so that everyone understands their role and can feel part of, and wanted in, the community.

We can now look at the subject of sneak thieves, vandalism and trespassers.

Sneak Thieves

It was probably the high-security measures used by the car manufacturers that made the sneak thief become more prominent, as it is now virtually impossible to steal new-generation vehicles because of the immobilizers and management systems built into them. Therefore, for those criminals who originally thrived on the stolen vehicles market it became incredibly difficult to take cars without getting access to the keys. For this reason thieves would target homes and try to 'sneak' into the house when it was left open, such as during the day, and try to take car keys alongside any other small valuable items.

Sadly the only way to truly and effectively beat the sneak thief is by always keeping the external doors locked and the windows closed but this can be an irritation to many people at home. Interestingly, the vast majority of intruder alarms feature a chime facility. This is a function, by which, even when the alarm is unset, i.e. switched off, the external doors, if fitted with sensors, can emit a chime if they are opened. It means the doors do not need to be locked but only kept closed. A sneak thief hearing the chime is always spooked by the sound of the chime as they do not know who may have heard this audible tone or if other signals have been sent elsewhere. For this reason they will certainly no longer wish to risk entering the home. The chime facility is a good option in these circumstances.

For those who do not have an intruder alarm installed it is possible to purchase inexpensive door switches with batteries that are self-contained and do the same thing. In other words they monitor an unlocked door becoming opened in which case they will emit a warning tone to 'spook' an unauthorized person entering the house.

We need to remember that a sneak thief is a sneak thief and a burglar is a burglar. They do not set out to be anything else, so we need to ensure that we have security in place to stop them entering our lives and giving them a chance to become more extreme. If they are confronted, they can become unpredictable. If their activities are bungled on our premises, we cannot be sure of how they will react. We do not want them to target us in the first place. Therefore, we are committed to having security at all material times.

It is fair to say that CCTV and monitoring systems that use cameras to capture images of areas around the perimeter of the home are becoming increasingly prominent in the residential sector. As they become more within the budget and running costs of the mainstream homeowner this will help to deter many bogus callers since the activities of these criminals, and their physical appearance and characteristics, will be recorded for evidential purposes. In fact they also help us combat vandalism as a part of our security measures.

Vandalism and Trespassers

We can define the vandal as someone who causes wilful damage. They can be a scourge to our security, particularly if these persons damage the fabric of our perimeter security, such as our fences and gates, or they break windows that give access to our home.

One of the reasons that vandalism occurs is that the criminal feels hostile towards the property owner and wants to devalue their property. In addition to having to repair the damage caused by a vandal, the whole atmosphere of the area becomes devalued and it gives the impression that people living in the neighbourhood do not treasure their homes.

Vandalism also suggests that the area is not well protected and can be unsafe. The result is that the local area becomes less used in and around the point of the damaged property. For this reason the damage should be repaired immediately, since the longer it is left, the more prone it becomes to further attack.

The implementation of CCTV and monitoring systems can help enormously to protect ourselves against vandalism or to capture video images of the culprits with a view to apprehending these persons and subsequently stopping their activities. This is all within our control.

Vandalism can start by committing the act of trespass. This is being present on land or invading the land of another without the consent of the owner. In fact the trespasser need not enter the land in person, as throwing an object on to the land of another can be classed as a trespass. In all cases it must be intentional and the trespasser must overstay their welcome.

We know that CCTV and the employment of monitoring by electronic security can help curtail these problems, so we can put certain practices in place. The other measures that are beyond our scope include education and ensuring that young vandals and trespassers recognize the difference between pranks and causing criminal damage to property or entering areas without the consent of the owner.

Before we go on to the next chapter, dealing with physical security, it is as well that we overview the subject of insurance requirements and burglary prevention by gathering our thoughts.

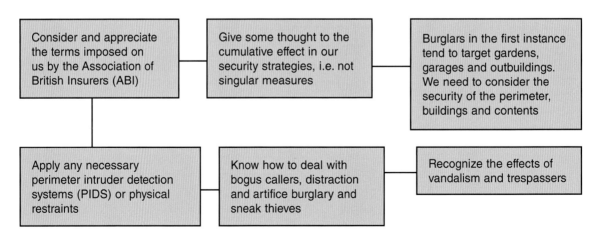

Architecture of requirements for insurance requirements and burglary prevention.

chapter three

Physical Security

In this chapter we are going to consider the use of physical security methods and how they need to be applied to help us improve our home security. We mean physical in the sense that we are referring to solid restraints or barriers. These restraints can be natural or man-made. In the first instance we are going to look at the considerations for natural features such as shrubs and trees and such. From that we will turn our attention to man-made barriers, such as fences, walls, and gates, and the other secure perimeter devices, such as doors and windows, plus shutters and grilles. The actual types of locking devices, components and safes that are available to us are also considered in this chapter.

We will conclude by looking at some legal issues and a range of other visible perimeter deterrents and methods.

PERIMETER SECURITY CONSIDERATIONS

The perimeter protection of our home is always the first obstacle that the criminal finds. Therefore it is to this that we must initially turn our attention. Of course good perimeter protection in isolation may never be sufficient to stop the determined criminal, and we must always bear in mind that the perimeter is only ever as strong as its weakest point. Nevertheless, the perimeter is important because it restricts criminal activity at the first stages of intrusion and by definition at the external confines of the home.

What we always accept is that, as we improve certain perimeter features, then other areas become more apparent in terms of vulnerability. For example, if we were to apply extremely high-security doors, windows and shutters to a home, it may then strike us that an intrusion could be possible by removing tiles from the roof of the house to gain access through the loft space. Prior to upgrading all of the doors, windows and shutters, we probably never gave a thought to the roof.

Although an intruder will never want to have to try to gain entry through a roof and loft space, it does happen occasionally to some homes that are in remote settings and where not overlooked by other dwellings. This illustrates that we are only capable of doing so much with the perimeter and we need to protect our property by taking account of proportionate probabilities and what are real-life risks for the home in question.

In the real world, any perimeter protection is better than nothing. However, although blinds fitted internally to a window together with a range of other obstacles placed awkwardly on the window sill may make it more difficult for an opportunist to break into a home easily and quietly through the window, it will certainly not stop a more determined person forcing their way past them.

Therefore our perimeter protection must be selected with a balanced view to ensure that an adequate level of protection is achieved.

SHRUBS AND TREES

The first part of our physical security measures checks must always start at the perimeter and what better point to start with than natural features.

Shrubs and trees around the perimeter of the home can actually be of benefit if they make access to the premises difficult. However, once this perimeter has been breached, they can then become of benefit to the criminal if they conceal areas to the home that can be attacked.

Shrubs near the windows or walkway can provide a place for the criminal to hide that is near to your house and trees can serve as a climbing aid to reach windows. To prevent burglars using your foliage against you, trim down your hedges to below the windows and your tree branches away from the windows. By planting trimmed bushes with thorns underneath your window, you will discourage burglars from hiding and sneaking in through the windows.

Planting prickly shrubs or trees around the perimeter of a property is a big deterrent. So, if plants or trees are used as a natural barrier, they must be kept well-pruned so that they do not block the view of the property.

A burglar trying to break in will be much happier if hidden by overgrown foliage. Therefore shrubbery, even around the front of a property, should be kept low and always below 1m.

So we can say that prickly planting is a visual deterrent and physical barrier that can complement other home security measures. It can be adopted to protect perimeters of your property, to form a barrier around drainpipes or beneath ground-floor windows, etc., making entry more difficult.

The following guide may help you to select a particular type that can be of benefit to your own property.

- *Pyracantha* Large evergreen shrubs suitable for wall training or hedge. Thorny branches. Grows up to 10m tall.
- *Hippophae rhamnoides* This large shrub has excellent thorns and provides superb cover.
- *Berberis ottawensis superba* A barbed plant capable of growing to 2m in height.
- *Berberis stenophylla* Has long arching prickly branches and grows to a height of 2.5m.
- *Berberis juliana* A prickly evergreen shrub that grows up to 1.8m tall.
- *Ulex europaeus* Viciously spiny it grows to a height of 1.8m tall.
- *Mahonia bealei* winter sun A prickly evergreen shrub that reaches a height of 1.8m.
- *Crataegus monogyna* A common hawthorn that forms an impenetrable thorny hedge. Fast-growing and must be pruned to required height.

Hedge obscuring a property. In practice this hedge actually obscures a patio door, a kitchen window and a rear external door at ground-floor level, which are all located just over the other side of the hedge. Therefore, it is a severe risk to security as it enables a criminal to be able to work unobserved when attempting to make a forced entry through any of those easily accessible points.

- *Ilex* A holly especially used for hedging.

Climbing and rambling roses are useful to give added protection to walls and fences. A wide selection is available with heights varying:

- *Rosa rugosa rubra-crimson* A densely prickly rose for hedges that grows up to 2m tall.
- *Rosa blanc double de coubert* A fragrant, old-fashioned rose that is densely prickly for hedges or individual shrubs and grows up to 2m high.

Of course we need to adopt more security measures than can be offered by prickly plants and natural features used alone. For sure we do not always have the benefit of time on our side when we want to grow prickly plants or such and then wait for them to develop properly. Equally there are many instances where we can simply not use natural features in isolation, so we also need to turn to a range of man-made physical security restraints.

FENCES, WALLS AND GATES

It is fences, walls and gates that form the essential perimeter of our home, no matter what sort of environment we live in.

Fences and Walls

The idea of a fence or wall is to:

- Define a particular area.
- Control entry to, and exit from, the area.

So we can say the same for a wall or fence as both restrict or prevent access through a boundary and they are free-standing. However, a fence tends to be lighter in its construction whilst a wall would, in general terms, be a more solid feature.

Both fences and walls vary enormously in terms of their height and construction, but to some extent or other they do provide privacy and prevent trespassing, even though in some instances they are easily circumnavigated or scaled. Nevertheless they do tell the observer that access is restricted, the owner is interested in marking out their property and the scaling of these barriers should not be attempted as a matter of course. So they do issue a warning to an intruder by their very presence.

In the strictest sense of the word, walls block vision through them better than fences because they are more solid, but of course we do still have an overlap of definitions.

Walls and fences therefore vary from light-weight, flimsy constructions that may be easily stepped over, to maximum security, extended height, electrified fences protected by alarms and ringed by barbed wire. Of course somewhere in the middle we have a range of aesthetically designed domestic products that may have an element of deterrent as perimeter security physical devices that are principally adopted to define the homeowners' property and area.

Walls can be built from extremely strong building materials, such as bricks, stone or concrete, and yet still not look out of place in the domestic environment, whilst offering good security and perimeter protection.

Nevertheless what value do we get from installing fences and walls, depending on their type and size, and what do we also need to consider in our assessments?

As a guide to selection for security purposes:

- Fences and walls signify a controlled area by their boundaries.
- They make the carrying of tools to the area and the taking of goods from the area, more difficult for the criminal.
- Intruders are concerned about becoming trapped within the area bordered by the fence or wall. Also, the apprehension of intruders becomes more possible as it slows up their escape.
- Fences of vertical-panel construction and with a lack of horizontal cross-member beams are more difficult to climb. Palisade

fencing is used in high volume for homes as it uses vertical, upright building materials that may be wood, metal or concrete with slots in-between to allow the wind to pass through the fence.

- Vehicles can only enter the area by using an authorized route.
- Security systems' monitoring becomes possible in a controlled area not open to public access.
- Considerations are fence and wall height, and construction, which must be acceptable to the local authority and take into account neighbours' rights. There may also be a need for maintenance and upkeep of the fence or wall.
- But beware that high fences and walls, if sited badly, can also be used by criminals to conceal themselves. It may seem a good idea to have a high wall around our perimeter to keep intruders out, but it can be used by criminals to hide their activities once they are on the inside of it! Also, criminals can of course hide behind solid fences and walls, so make sure you take this into account in your analysis.

It is fair to say that walls tend to be built or constructed at the actual home site, whereas fences can be delivered to the site in sections, in parts or as panels, and then erected. Therefore a wall may be more purpose-constructed, whilst a fence can be pre-fabricated; so fences are more easily erected.

Fences and walls are supported by gates to enable access to be made through them.

Gates

Gates are used to allow entrance to, and exit from, the home or garden bordering the property. If we were only to think purely in terms of security, then the gate would need to offer exactly the same level of security that has been afforded to the fence or wall it serves or it becomes the weakest link. However, in practice this is rarely the case for all gates.

We find many open drives at the front of properties and no gate in existence, even though the home may have good perimeter walls or fences. This is because the front is often an area that is overlooked by other houses, so is not normally a target for the criminal. However, the same property may well have a back gate to restrict access to the rear of the home, which may not be overlooked in the same way. Therefore the gate, or the need for a gate, will always be dictated by the position it needs to be installed to serve the best access point to the property. So we apply different requirements to what we know historically as 'front' and 'back' gates. That is on the proviso that the front of the property is overlooked by other houses and the back is more vulnerable as it is not overlooked.

We can therefore conclude that the gate should be considered in our security assessment in the same way as the wall or fence it serves, if it must be fitted at a position that could be readily targeted by the intruder or used as an entry and exit route to and from the home and surrounding area.

Gates should only be installed at points that are not vulnerable in terms of their location. If this cannot be avoided, then they are not to be the weak link, so need to retain the same level of security in terms of the integrity of the bordering fences and walls.

If a high gate is not wanted but the homeowner is concerned that a low gate can be easily climbed or vaulted, an option is to install a horizontal cross-member at just above head height over the gate position. This makes it difficult to climb over the gate because the cross-member acts as an obstruction. It also slows up the escape of an intruder who may be trying to run from the area and wanting to vault the fence without having to slow up as they approach the closed gate.

The figure on page 38 illustrates a home with a high-quality gate system for both persons and vehicles. It will also be noted that it has fences of the same constructional form.

GUIDE TO RESIDENTIAL HOME FENCES

Palisade
These use vertical panels with a small gap between each panel. They are aesthetically pleasing and tend to be of wood construction for homes, although other materials such as metal or concrete can be found.

Privacy
These use panels with no gap between them to enclose the property. They are intended to not allow any vision to be made through them, so need to be at least of head height.

Lattice
These are semi-private but are quite appealing in terms of appearance. They use crisscross patterns of wood with holes in between, so can be seen through.

Picket
A type of palisade fence, normally of wood. They can also be concave at the top by using panels of different height to give a varying height pattern to improve their aesthetics.

Slat
These use horizontal panels to give a distinct appeal. For security there must be no gap between the panels to stop intruders climbing them easily.

Basket Weave
As the name suggests they use horizontally weaved thin panels. Consideration must be given to their construction to stop intruders climbing them easily by getting footholds on the weaving of the panels.

Post and Rail
Very easy to install, they are of an open construction, using minimal numbers of posts and rails. They are easy to climb or get access through but do at least mark out the privacy area of the home.

Chain Link
Available in a range of materials, including galvanized steel and plastic. They are strong, cost-effective and rather difficult to climb.

Mesh Panel
Similar to chain link, they are available in a wide range of materials and mesh patterns. They are strong and allow vision to be made through them.

Ornamental
These are intended for appearance with wrought iron design popular. They offer little protection but do establish the boundaries of the home.

To the observer this all suggests that the homeowner has pride in their home and furthermore is prepared to invest in good security via substantial perimeter protection. Not only that but as these gates and the fencing can be seen through, they do not allow an intruder to hide. An intruder cannot, therefore, be in a position to attack the windows or doors of the home whilst being concealed from other neighbours or passers-by.

An unwelcome caller to the home would be deterred by the presence of such perimeter gate systems, whereas a welcome visitor would be reassured by them.

High-quality gates and fencing.

DOORS, WINDOWS, SHUTTERS AND GRILLES

These form the fabric of the home in terms of openings. If breached, they provide easy access to the intruder.

Doors are the first natural target area for the criminal since they obviously come to ground level and make access to and from the home convenient for the criminal in exactly the same way that they allow ease of entry and exit to the homeowner.

Patio doors and French doors (sometimes called French windows) are particular targets as, in general, they have less secure locks than main external doors and they are often located at the more vulnerable rear of the premises. Many patio doors are sliding, so attacks on them may lead to attempts to lift them up and off their runners.

French doors are double leaf so are always less secure than single leaf doors because they present two targets to the intruder.

Doors and Windows

If we look at the security guides for the selection of doors and windows we will find that the selection depends on a number of issues including the following:

- The location of the door/window.
- The location of the property.
- The value of the property.
- The desirability of the goods or information in the property.
- The risks relating to the loss of goods.
- The use of additional security measures and systems.

Doors

Taking doors first, let us look at how we can offer essential security to an external door by referring to the figure on page 39. These are general aspects, as we deal with the specific requirements for front and back doors later in this chapter.

The door illustrated has been fitted with a mortise sash-lock. A mortise sash-lock is actually the same as a mortise deadlock but it also has a handle in order to open the door when the sash-lock has been unlocked and retracted. It should be a five-lever lock for insurance purposes and be BS 3621 (European Standard EN 12209).

Mortise sash-locks and deadlocks are fitted flush within the material of the door and frame, so have great strength. Note, however, that you need to avoid using rim latch Yale-type locks (night-latch locks) as the main locking device because, as the name suggests, these are only mounted on the rim, i.e. the surface

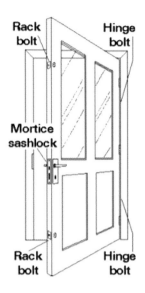

Rim lock. Avoid the use of rim locks where high levels of security are required, as they only mount on the surface of the door, so lack the strength of mortise locks. Rim locks can be fitted on internal doors or for low security risk outbuildings.

Door security.

or face of the door and frame. Therefore they lack the strength of the mortise (sometimes referred to as mortice) sash-lock and deadlock components, which are sunk into the door and frame.

Once again, we will look further into the use of locks on doors to satisfy insurance requirements and different levels of security,

later in this chapter.

The use of rack bolts and hinge bolts is also illustrated. The rack bolts should be installed in pairs, some 150mm from the top and bottom of the doors.

The use of multiple locking devices always makes it very difficult to force a door open. This is because pressure needs to be exerted on the door at a number of different points or throughout the total length of the door at the same time, which makes charging at it or impacting it extremely difficult.

A door with two locks fitted, e.g. one at the top and one at the bottom, is considerably more secure than a door with only one lock fitted central to the door, as both locks need impacting simultaneously to force them open.

Hinge bolts always further enhance the door's strength around the hinge areas and make it awkward to prise the door upwards from the frame.

It is also more complicated to break open a door if it is outward opening, since it needs to be prised open rather than forcing it open by impacting it. To prise a secure door open can be extremely challenging.

Door security is further improved by fitting a door viewer (spy hole) and a door chain or door limiter. These allow the homeowner to deal

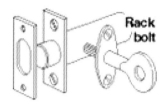

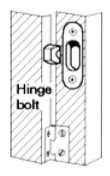

Rack bolt and hinge bolt. Rack bolts should be installed at the top and bottom of the door, and hinge bolts used to support and improve the security of the door hinges.

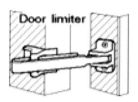

Door viewer, door chain and door limiter. Doors are the first target area for criminals and the natural approach point for the bogus caller so need special attention.

The sketches shown on this page are time-honoured in the industry. These drawings illustrate a number of component devices used for door security purposes. The devices will continue to have an ongoing use for the foreseeable future.

with callers while retaining a level of security. They do, of course, tend to be used on front doors.

On the subject of front doors, letter boxes and plates can be used by criminals to extract goods that are in close proximity to the door, especially door keys and car keys, or to work vulnerable locking devices from the inside. Criminals use hooks or wires to grab or to fish for keys or small valuables and to then draw these items through the letter box. Letter plates, therefore, should conform to British Standards for construction and positioning. They should be installed no closer than 400mm

from the door lock and not be fitted to the bottom rail of the door. An internal cover plate offers additional security, as do letter baskets, as they help to prevent keys or small valuables being pulled through them. Letter baskets can, in fact, help criminals to steal mail but this can be avoided by fitting a flap to the bottom of the basket.

Clearly the security of the door is not governed entirely by the locks, as the frame must be sound and the door suitable for external use. Wooden, hollow core doors are unacceptable for external use. The door should be of substantial solid construction and be at least 44mm thick to support the mortise lock and hung on three strong 100mm hinges. Two-hinge bolts should be used to support the hinge side.

The door must be inherently strong and the frame should have a rebate of at least 18mm. Any recessed or decorative panels used in the door should be a minimum of 9mm thick.

It is also worth considering fitting a metal strip on the frame side to support the strike box, or a bar to support the frame on the hinge side. These are often referred to as 'London' or 'Birmingham' bars. If the door is not particularly substantial in construction, consider fitting a sheet steel plate or steel door reinforcement on the outside to cover the lock area.

Timber frames should be sound and securely bolted or screwed to the supporting walls every 600mm around the whole frame.

Doors with glazed panels are not as secure as solid doors, hence the need for a deadlock. Ordinary or toughened glass panels can be replaced with laminated glass, which is effectively two pieces of glass bonded together with a sheet of laminate, as they offer much greater resistance to attack. Laminated glass cracks on impact but the pieces stay in position. A further option is toughened glass, which is far stronger than standard glass, or wired safety glass, which has wire embedded in it and behaves like laminated glass if broken. Glass panels should be fitted from the inside so that the putty or beading cannot be removed from the outside.

In order to address the need for door security, we now have an enormous range of doors and frames available to us. These include UPVC, PVCu, aluminium, timber and composite materials but some of these are unsuitable for retro-fit security devices and changes to the original design may invalidate an existing warranty or possibly damage the integral locking assembly. However, modern door designs from reputable manufacturers do take into account the homeowner's security needs. Therefore, such door designs usually incorporate deadlock shoot bolts or a multi-point locking system that throws a number of bolts from the door into the frame, so no additional locking devices are needed. UPVC and PVCu doors may also have steel inserts within the panels to resist efforts by intruders to burn holes through them using hand-held blowtorches.

Remember, if buying a purpose-designed door, check the locking options available, as what are 'standard' locking devices for one supplier or manufacturer may be 'optional' for another.

Note also that if the supplier is not registered in the Fenestration Self-Assessment Scheme (FENSA), then any double-glazing work needs to be certified by the local building control officers to prove it meets the Building Regulations. The scheme was set up by the Glass and Glazing Federation (GGF), with government encouragement, in response to new Building Regulations.

Locking options on patio doors and French doors are of particular importance because of the security issues surrounding these openings.

Patio Doors and French Doors

These are often vulnerable points because they are installed at the rear of the home to give access to areas that are intended to be rather private for the homeowner and not overlooked by neighbours.

Intruders will always attempt to enter by patio doors or French doors, if possible. If they have to gain access by a different point, such as a window, they will then try to force open either the patio door or French doors, as these present an easier and alternative escape route and it allows them to run quickly from the home if confronted.

Remember, criminals do not want to have to try to scramble through a window to exit a home especially if being chased.

A number of options are available to improve the locking security of these openings, depending on the materials from which they are constructed. The rack bolt is a further method.

It is possible that patio-door runners can be

fitted with spacers in the frame above the door to stop them being lifted up off their runners or a bar placed to stop the door sliding along for internally sliding assemblies. An old style of protection for internally sliding patio doors was to place a long length of wood in the runners to stop the door being slid along.

Intruder alarms, when installed in the home, should always include protection of external doors, including patio doors and French doors. If a purpose-designed intruder alarm is not installed, a basic self-contained alarm can be fitted on these openings that will, at the very least, give a measure of additional protection to the mechanical locking devices. These will give an audible warning if these doors are forced open.

A variant patio door is the barn or Dutch door, which is effectively a two-part door comprising two openers, one above the other. It is necessary to consider both halves of these doors when carrying out the locking and physical security measures for them to ensure it is not possible for an intruder to force open one half, even though the other half remains firmly secure.

Windows

Originally any vulnerable windows in the home were also protected by intruder alarm systems. The alarm system protected the window by the fitting of switches that sensed the window being opened. Alternatively, vibration or seismic sensors detected impact on the window, or glass break sensors detected the glass being broken. However, this is now no longer the case as far as standard practice is concerned for houses, since the physical strength and security attributes of windows has moved on enormously. Also, the fitting of wiring around windows and alarm devices on the windows itself were never particularly welcome when it came to aesthetics. Therefore, domestic windows are not now normally fitted with alarm devices unless there is a particular security need or unless they are windows in a vulnerable perimeter outer area, such as a utility room, where aesthetics are not quite so important.

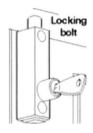

Locking bolt, patio door lock and mortise/mortice security bolt.

The security of modern windows now includes a range of locking devices with keys and limiters. An intruder will obviously be reluctant to try to gain entry through a secure and substantial new-generation front window with only a small opener at the top of the frame. However, they will certainly still be prepared to at least try to force entry through windows that are not overlooked by other houses, or are sited at low level, if other easier routes into the targeted home are unavailable. It follows that any vulnerable windows in the home for security purposes must always be of high security and of modern architecture.

Although it is often the case that the weakest point of any window is the glass, it is also fair to say that criminals do not want to have to smash the glass of the window and then climb through. They may cut themselves, leaving behind DNA, but not only that, they much prefer to have an easy, large, clear opening available to them.

Although criminals do not want to have to go to the extent of removing a complete window pane from a frame, they may be able to do this with externally beaded units. The question we must ask ourselves is, if a pane of glass needed to be replaced, how easy could it be taken out. This answer will let us know just how easy a criminal could remove the pane from the frame. If this is a concern, elect to have modern internally beaded windows only, so that the pane of glass cannot be removed from the outside but needs to be taken out when access has been made to the inside of the home.

However, there are solutions to the problem of externally beaded units if the homeowner wants to retain those windows. A common solution is to use a double-sided adhesive tape, which bonds the window to the frame. If using this method it is essential that good bonding is achieved because there is no practical way by which the glass can be checked as secure, apart from taking the beading off and checking.

A different solution is to use purpose-designed metal locks that can be fitted easily and retrospectively to all externally glazed windows. The metal base is bonded to the glass with a special adhesive and a clamp is installed and adjusted to suit the window-frame profile. It gives a visible deterrent to any would-be burglar not to attempt to remove the beads and can be inspected easily. In effect the glass is mechanically locked into the frame so it cannot be removed without smashing the glass. This solution is readily applied to those existing externally beaded windows that the homeowner, for any particular reason, may not wish to change.

Although it is not a particularly difficult or noise-creating task for the determined criminal to remove the beading from ordinary externally beaded units, it has always been a rather more difficult and time-consuming exercise to remove the beading and putty from traditional wooden windows. Therefore, when upgrading to modern UPVC and PVCu windows from wooden units, ensure that increased security protection is being offered in regard to both removing the window pane in total and also being able to break out the glass. We can refer back to the options we have for glass, as already mentioned for doors.

If it is decided to upgrade an older window design that has opening panes and perhaps only single glazing, there are a number of options available to improve its security. These include standard rack bolts, locking bolts or mortise security bolts.

In fact there are other locks and devices that can be attached to the handle itself to stop it being easily opened if an intruder smashes out a section of glass and then tries to open the window by reaching through to the handle inside. These include screw-cap fittings or devices using fixing pins. These all stop the handle being easily opened, as they need some type of key or tool to release these locks or devices in order to turn the handle. They do offer good resistance to someone on the outside of the house trying to reach through a broken section of glass, although they can never be a true security solution to compare with the protection offered by the new generation of high-quality designed windows with their superior glass and locking devices.

So let us add that for any window on the ground floor, and for other windows that are easily accessible, key-operated locks are an essential feature. Window handles should be multi-locking, with shoot bolts into the frame.

Shutters and Grilles

The security value of shutters and grilles is well demonstrated by their widespread use in the commercial sector. However, as physical barriers they are often overlooked in the residential market, despite the valuable role they have to play in the protection of particularly vulnerable doors and windows.

Roller shutters are available in a range of sizes. They are incredibly robust and can be mounted on the outside of the door or window but in some instances may need planning permission. In terms of aesthetics they are not suitable to everyone's taste but they can be used, as needs dictate, if security is the overriding issue.

Security grilles for the home come in a range of forms, the most prominent being concertina, sliding or retractable. This means they are moveable to enable easy access to be made through them once they have been unlocked. Security grilles of traditional lattice appearance can be installed externally or internally, and either be secured to the framework of the home or fixed into the opening on all four sides.

Concertina grilles can be installed internally and are aesthetically pleasing. When opened they may be tucked away neatly behind curtains or vertical blinds. These security grilles are an excellent visual deterrent, as well as a physical one, as the majority of would-be burglars, when seeing a grille in the window, are no longer keen to try to break in. They can be matched to the window frames or any colour scheme of the home. Concertina grilles can in fact also be used to protect doors, hatches, car ports and any other openings. All grilles come in a range of security grades from basic through to insurance-tested, heavy duty with specific locking mechanisms.

In some instances there may be no requirement for a window to open, such as in basements and cellar, but the window is only required to allow natural light to enter the area. In these circumstances, fixed grilles or steel bars may be used across the opening, as security takes precedence over aesthetics.

LOCKS AND LOCKING DEVICES

Although there are a huge variety of types of lock available to us for the many different applications we use them for, we will find in practice that they all very much offer different levels of security and strength. However, for certain critical applications, such as external

Home security grilles. Security grilles installed either externally or internally may be concertina, sliding or retractable, so enable easy access to be made through them when unlocked.

doors, it will be found that the insurance companies specify that the door locks are to be BS 3621 'Thief resistant lock assembly. Key egress'.

Locks that have been approved to this noted standard are able to bear the British Standard Kite Mark BS 3621 to prove that samples of them have gone through a vigorous testing procedure to make them very secure against any person trying to break the lock. Such tests include drilling, sawing and using a measured level of force to open the lock. Therefore the user is assured of the capability of the lock to be able to perform to the demanding standards of duty required of it.

So from this we can say:

- For many years BS 3621 has been a well-established product standard for thief-resistant locks in the UK.
- Insurance companies specify that security locks are tested to BS 3621 to comply with the requirements of insurance cover. It follows the same classification and performance testing within Europe as BS EN 12209.

We know that the front door and the back door, plus any other external doors including patio doors and French windows, have long been a target for intruders. Therefore let us now overview the locks and locking devices for these openings to give us a high level of security, bearing in mind that the different insurers will place different requirements on us. The boxes show the mandatory requirements, i.e. what must be fitted as a minimum to achieve a high level of security plus the additional options available to us, i.e. extra locking devices to even further support the mandatory devices.

This illustrates just how safety becomes a consideration alongside security, and the reasons why front and back door locking systems differ. It is not the case we want to compromise our security but we also need to know the ways we can safely exit our homes.

If we are to purchase new-generation doors from a reputable source, then it becomes

BS3621:2007

BS 3621 kite mark. Locks bearing the British Standard Kite Mark BS 3621 have been proved to perform to clearly defined requirements for security.

GUIDE TO LOCKING DEVICES – EXTERNAL DOORS

Front Door

Mandatory

Install a BS 3621 insurance-rated five-lever mortise deadlock plus a rim lock 'night latch' (Yale lock).
Note: Night latch is the correct terminology for what most people call a Yale or rim lock. It is simply a latch operated by a turn from one side and by a key from the other side. Sometimes they are called slam locks, due to the reason that once the door is closed behind you, a key is needed to come back through the door.

Additional Options

Add hinge bolts, as appropriate.

Back Door and Other External Doors

Mandatory

Install a BS 3621 insurance-rated five-lever sash-lock.

Additional Options

Add rack bolts, hinge bolts, locking bolts, patio door locks and mortise security bolts, as appropriate.
Note: For safety reasons, in the event of a fire the occupants must be able to exit the premises quickly, but locating keys and engaging them can cause a delay. Fire-safety officers may advise against the use of using the front door deadlock when the house is occupied but only to use it when the house is vacated, hence the need for the night latch only to be used during the time the house is occupied. This illustrates why we have different requirements for front and back and other external doors and the lack of rack bolts, etc. on front doors.

easy to meet the requirements for security and safety, as they will incorporate modern flush-mounted multi-point locking systems specifically approved by the insurance industry. Interesting is the fact that some insurers now accept BS 3621 rim automatic deadlocks on traditional front doors without any extra locking devices. Being surface-mounted rim locks, these are not as strong as mortise locks but they allow easier exiting of the front door to be made in an emergency because, although lockable from the outside, they do have a simple turnable knob on the inside.

Having considered locking devices on external doors, we can now turn our attention to the more general main locks and locking devices used in and around the home and how we may apply them.

An example of a digital lock, which may also be called a push-button lock, is illustrated. These lock types are extremely convenient because the user does not need a key to

GUIDE TO MAIN LOCKS AND LOCKING DEVICES

Mortise Locks: Flush-Mounted Devices
Being sunk into the frame and door they are known as flush-mounted. They possess great strength, so provide high levels of security. The deadlock facility used on the mortise lock has no spring action, so the latch-bolt is projected and becomes locked by the action of the key. Sashlocks also include an additional spring-return handle to hold the door closed when the door is unlocked.

Rim Locks: Surface-Mounted Devices
Also called Yale or night-latch locks. Being mounted on the rim or surface of the frame and door they are not as strong and secure as mortise locks, but they do allow quick exiting to be made through them.

Plunger Locks: Installed on Cabinet Doors
These engage a plunger, which is projected when the lock is engaged and retracted by a spring when unlocked. Other versions of plunger locks are electrified and 'shoot out' the plunger to secure doors or shutters when subject to an electrical signal.

Lever Locks: Widespread Use on Internal Doors and Windows
These are simply a lock that incorporates a key in the handle (or knob) that can lock the latch-bolt in position, as and when required. Otherwise the latch may be spring-loaded to allow the door or window to be held closed but be unlocked under normal circumstances.

Bolts: Steel Bolts Can be Installed on the Inside of Doors, Windows and Shutters
Locking bolts, mortise bolts and rack bolts, together with standard sliding bolts can be found either surface- or flush-mounted.

Digital Locks: May Also be Called Combination Locks
Use a combination code rather than a key to operate the lock. Often found on internal doors as the user does not need to carry a key around to operate them. They can also be found in an electrified version in order to be opened automatically from a remote point using an intercom or access control system.

Padlocks: Available in a Huge Variety and with Differing Levels of Security
Selection must take into account width, case length and shackle. Can use either keys or digital combination. Outside use and how often it will be operated, and the goods it must protect, also govern padlock selection.
U-bolts are available as specialist padlocks to secure particular and valuable goods, such as cycles and gardening equipment.

Chains: Normally Used with Padlocks
Steel chains are almost impossible to cut through without specialist tools.

Digital lock.

Padlock (traditional style).

Block padlock.

operate them and they have a facility to allow the code or combination to be changed if the user suspects that a person not authorized to open the lock has obtained information as to the code.

The lock is made up of two parts. The code lock is fitted on one side of the door and a thumb turn is fitted on the other side of the door, so the house or protected area can be easily exited.

Padlocks come in a wide range of variants and security levels.

The block padlock has a rotating shackle, which offers rather better protection against attack by criminals, as it is better protected by the enclosure of the lock casing.

Locks and locking devices form a huge subject and there are many things we need to consider. Some general observations can help us to select appropriate devices. So let us overview the subject by thinking in terms of lock security and anti-shim devices.

Lock Security and Anti-Shim Devices

There are many aspects that we need to consider when we think of lock security, but let us remind ourselves of some of the more significant things.

In the selection process for our locking devices we must take account of the standards that the lock satisfies, the number of levers the lock may have, alongside its declared strength and resistance to attack by criminals or vandals. Also, the lock needs to be able to resist the weather if used externally.

We may also want to know how many combinations it may have; in other words, how many locks are made that use exactly the same key as that of our own lock. Most locking devices are in fact time-honoured, so do tend to be reliable in construction, being built with precision to fine limits.

Locking devices also evolve, so manufacturers are able to develop and further improve their products to upgrade on the existing strength and protection offered by them.

Locks may also be operated by a key or they can be of combination lock form and operated by a number or code. Both types have advantages and disadvantages.

Keys can, of course, be lost or the user may forget to bring along the key, whereas this cannot happen with combination locks; but with these locks, the user has to be vigilant and not let others see the combination being entered.

Remember also that the duplication of keys or the disclosure of combinations for all locks can be a security problem, particularly for gated communities and buildings with shared entrances. In these instances, patent protect systems are needed, as these stop illegal duplication. This means that borrowed keys cannot be copied without authorization, so system security is unlikely to be compromised. It also eliminates the risk of ex-tenants getting access to buildings.

In all cases we should always mount or apply locks and devices to sound surfaces. Also, flush-mounted products are always superior, as they are more difficult to attack. In addition, all locks are more difficult to get access to and attack if shrouds can be placed over them to stop levers being used on them to force them open.

We should also try to use locks that have stood the test of time in similar locking applications and in doing so have been successful. Allied to this, we need to be alert to the developments of locks as the market for things such as PVCu doors grows and so do the methods used to attack the locking cylinders on the doors.

Anti-snap cylinders are designed so that the front of the cylinder deliberately comes away under attack. The remaining part of the cylinder sits beneath the surface of the door skin, which makes the actual lock mechanism extremely difficult to attack.

In practice, therefore, lock manufacturers are acutely aware of the growing demands from homeowners for higher levels of protection against new forms of cylinder-manipulation attack. Therefore, we will see claims from the manufacturers of locks that their products are anti-drill, anti-snap, anti-bump and even anti-pick and, to some extent, they will be.

Picking of locks is, of course, an old practice, so perhaps we may want to know how vulnerable our locks may be to picking. Lock picking is the manipulation of a lock's components in order to open it without the need for a key. Although we see it as an act of criminal intent, it is actually something that a locksmith must

be capable of doing. Therefore, we now have many sophisticated tools to do this because a locksmith must be able to continue to carry out this practice.

Of course picking may also be practised by criminals who are determined to find a means of opening locks other than by the use of more brutal means and who can get access to the same picking tools as a professional and legitimate locksmith. This all suggests that we can never really rely on one level of security alone when considering our perimeter protection.

A further thing we need to know something about is shimming. Remember that there are effectively two types of bolts used for most door applications; these are the latch-bolt and the dead-bolt. They can be distinguished as the latch-bolt has a bevelled face, whereas the face on a dead-bolt is square.

The latch-bolt allows a door to be slammed, so is spring-loaded. So when the door on which the latch-bolt is mounted is in the process of closing, the latch-bolt automatically retracts. When the door is fully closed, the latch springs back securing the door. The latch-bolt is obviously convenient because it automatically locks when it is pulled closed and no additional effort with a key is required. However, it lacks high security because the latch-bolt can be forced back by the insertion of a thin shim, such as a plastic credit card or knife inserted between the face plate of the lock and the strike. Anti-shim devices may be added to the basic latch-bolt to counter such attacks as they are designed to prevent the latch-bolt being depressed once the door is closed.

From this we may conclude that any locking mechanism that relies on spring pressure alone to hold the lock in place is vulnerable to shimming unless they are protected by anti-shim devices.

Safes form the next part of our investigations into physical security measures, as these are robust units that incorporate true secure locking devices.

SAFES

I suppose we can say that safes have the highest physical protection of anything we can think of. Although not everyone may feel that they have a need for a safe, we all probably have a need for what we can call a 'safe area', i.e. somewhere we can safely keep valuables, including cash and credit cards, together with keys and important documents, such as a will or the deeds to a house.

Thinking further to the use of safes, key cabinets are available to retain keys in a secure and convenient way for those houses that have a high volume of keys.

People go on holiday and often hide things in the loft of the house or at some other obscure point as a precaution against burglary. However, for purposes of security a more organized way of doing this is to have a small domestic safe large enough to hold valuables and documents plus things like laptop computers.

A further option is to simply have a clearly defined but concealed 'safe area'. For example, a small box can be set into a wall and then concealed behind the face of a non-working electrical socket that to the intruder looks like a working electrical point but in practice is simply a decoy. This hidden box can hold small valuables. For larger items, a removable panel can be placed in the back of a cupboard to cover a much larger box that can contain an array of valuables. The means of hiding valuables in a controlled safe area is therefore endless and only limited by the imagination of the user.

For those of us who want to purchase a safe or cabinet for the home, they are available in a range of sizes to meet almost any budget. They offer various locking options including key, electronic digital keypad or mechanical dial combination. These are cash rated to cover money or valuables up to a given level or grade of the safe used.

If high security must prevail, then Eurograde safes, which are tested and comply with the most stringent European Security standard EN 1143–1, are available and approved by all of the major insurance companies. Eurograde ratings are formed from seven levels with the lowest being Grade 0 and the highest being Grade VI or Grade 6. Having a certified Eurograde safe ensures that leading UK insurance companies will normally cover for the loss or theft of cash or valuables to the value designated to the grade of the safe used.

To comply with the standard EN 1143–1, sample safes are tested by attacking for partial and complete access and on satisfactory completion are certified to an appropriate grade.

Although it may be the case that safes offer us increased security, it is still to be understood that:

- Your insurance company may require you to purchase from a specific manufacturer.
- The insurance premium for home contents should decrease in cost.
- Certain safes protect against fire and burglary, as they offer fire protection for paper.

Safety cabinets are rather different and specific to the product. For instance, firearms and weapons need to be held in carefully controlled cabinets, which will be specified and checked by the police authorities.

We tend to site safes and security cabinets in areas that prevent them from being normally visible, but in the next section we are going to consider some items that are more visible by their very nature.

VISIBLE AND PERIMETER DETERRENTS

Before we can move on to consider a few other options available to us as visible physical security barrier items we just need to give some thought to the legal issues that control their use:

Duty of Care to Trespassers

Anyone who owns, or controls, property has a legal duty of care to protect people on the property from foreseeable harm. This duty even extends to people on the property without permission, to include burglars and vandals. A householder can therefore be sued for damages under the Occupier's Liability Act 1984 if a burglar is injured whilst on their property. The test would be whether the householder could have predicted that a trespasser was likely to be injured. For instance, if broken glass has deliberately been placed at a likely entry-point, then any subsequent injury suffered will have been entirely foreseeable.

Discharging the Duty

A householder may be able to discharge this duty by warning trespassers of the hazard or by discouraging them from coming onto the property. This could be done by putting up a sign that warns of the danger.

> ### Attention   Glass on Wall   Keep Out

Discharging the duty. Warning sign.

This would be intended to act in such a way so as to not invite trespassers to risk hurting themselves. If a householder was sued, the court would then consider all of the circumstances of the case before deciding whether the householder was, indeed, liable for damages.

It is a fact that the Criminal Justice Act 2003 provides some protection to householders. If a trespasser suffers an injury during the course of a crime, for which they are subsequently convicted and for which they could be sent to prison, they will only be able to sue the householder if they get the court's permission to do so. The court is unlikely to grant permission unless the householder had taken grossly excessive steps or had not been acting to defend themselves, their family or property from an offence.

So with the legal side understood we can now overview our liabilities before going on to look at some interesting perimeter security measures.

Anti-Vandal Paint

This is also known as anti-climb, anti-intruder and anti-scale paint. As the names suggest, it is intended to prevent intruders from climbing up a surface where it has been applied and gaining access to a property. It usually comes in dark colours with black being prominent. Care should be taken to select a product that remains effective in both hot and cold weather conditions.

Once applied it does not dry and leaves a slippery surface that is very difficult to climb. Although it is not generally harmful, it will stain the clothes and the body of anyone who tries to climb it.

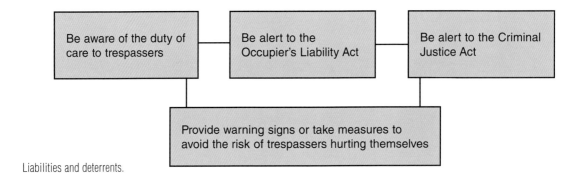

Liabilities and deterrents.

It can be used on many surfaces and is often applied to walls and drainpipes or any other surface or object that an intruder may attempt to climb. The paint is applied with a brush or by hand whilst wearing a protective glove. Once in place it should last for at least a year. However, the lifespan will depend on how often people attempt to climb the surface to which it has been applied.

But, let us go back a stage with respect to the legal issues, and the Occupier's Liability Act 1984. If anti-vandal paint has been applied to a wall and an intruder slips and injures themselves as a result, this is something that the householder could have predicted. Householders could also be caught up by the Highways Act 1980 if anti-vandal paint is used on a wall or surface that adjoins a public highway. The Highways Act states that care must be taken to avoid 'harm or injury' to any person or animal using the highway.

To discharge the duty of care owed to trespassers, householders must put up a warning sign if they are using anti-vandal paint. The sign or signs should be placed in the area where the paint is being used. Suppliers of anti-vandal paint will always sell warning signs. In addition the paint should only be applied to surfaces above 2m high, so that innocent passers-by do not come into contact with it.

Alternative Deterrents

Non-aggressive anti-climb systems can be attached to the tops of walls to prevent intruders gaining access in this way. For example, barriers made up of individual rotating cups attached to the top of a high wall are caused to spin when contacted and therefore stop an intruder from getting a hand-hold on the wall and climbing over.

Trellis fencing attached to the top of a high wall is also effective. This raises the height of the wall but is not strong enough to support an intruder's weight, so cannot be climbed.

Other methods are barbed wire, broken glass, nails, spikes and carpet grippers. These may not be inherently illegal but don't forget that there are restrictions on what householders can do, so careful consideration should be given to the legal position and the use of signs before any of these deterrent methods are used. Indeed a great many walls and gates with specific forms on the top are available to deter intruders from attempting to scale them. Those that have a mainstream and time-honoured use are worthy of attention.

In fact as far as standard practice goes, all gardens should ideally be surrounded by a well-built brick wall in the order of 2m high. Any side entrance to the property should also be protected by a fence or wall of the same height and any gate should be robust and have an efficient lock.

Gravel is interesting as it is not only an attractive home feature but an effective method of discouraging intruders because of the noise it makes when walked on. Also any vehicle approaching the house creates a major noise effect as it travels over a gravel based premises entry path or roadway.

So from this we can say that we cannot simply put spikes or such on our garden wall without looking at the wider picture. Life is not that easy.

The other major deterrent that generally makes noise of course is a dog!

However, it is down to the individual if they wish to take on the responsibility of owning a dog simply for the purposes of security. The homeowner would also need to ask themselves if the dog would always be available, including those times when they are away on holiday. For those who keep dogs as pets, they need to check the value of the dog in terms of security and if it can possibly provide an appropriate measure of security in the wider scheme of things. Also, if it started to bark regularly for no apparent reason, would this alienate the owner from the neighbours? Probably! So to check on the value of a dog for security purposes, make a careful analysis balanced against the side issues of ownership.

Dogs can, in fact, be seen as a progression from geese that were historically used on large estates to notify of persons approaching an area that was in need of protection.

Lighting, of course, is a further perimeter deterrent but we cover this in its own right in Chapter 5.

It is rather interesting that some of the physical security issues and perimeter protection methods we are faced with become more complicated as a result of progression in other ways. For instance, the widespread introduction of hand-held cordless power tools, such as drills and grinders, enable intruders to come better equipped to try to drill out locks or to cut through bars. Also, hand-held blow torches allow criminals to try to burn through plastic panels and through the covers of alarm-bell boxes. Bolt-cutters help intruders to conveniently tackle all manner of chains and locks.

So we will always need to face new challenges to counter the introduction of new and evolving practices.

A CONCLUDING THOUGHT

In terms of practical devices there truly is a multitude of things available to us, both natural and man-made, that we can use to enhance our physical security. Indeed there is a vast range of simple and basic practical restraints and deterrents that can be applied to our homes in a very easy way. These all give us an improvement in security and, even though it may only be marginal, it will always still have some measure of effect. Keep an open mind on what is available and the roles they have to play but to get the best from any products, never disregard the accompanying instructions for application of the goods.

chapter four

Electronic Security Systems

As we now know there are many options available to us that we can use to protect our family and possessions. So far we have looked at physical methods. Now we are going to investigate electronic ways of doing it.

Installing a security system is an effective method of protecting both ourselves and our homes and in this chapter we will consider all of the main areas of electronic security. We will start our investigations with intruder alarms because they form the nucleus of the electronic security systems industry.

INTRUDER ALARMS

Historically, intruder alarms were known to us as burglar alarms. However, they have become so technically advanced over the years that they are now often found connected to, or send messages to, other systems, such as lighting, fire detection, intercoms, CCTV links, or indeed mobile phones and computer networks. Yet the intruder alarm may still exist in its own right in a very basic way for those of us who want something of little complexity and simple home protection. So they are now known to us as intruder alarms rather than burglar alarms as a reflection on their more modern application and role.

So how do they work? Well, basically an intruder alarm system consists of three main elements:

- Detection devices.
- Control equipment.
- Signalling devices.

DETECTION DEVICES

These are devices that recognize intrusion or the presence of an intruder. The actual detection devices fall into two main protection categories known as perimeter or space. These items carry out the supervision of the protected property.

Perimeter protection devices are placed on openings such as doors or windows to detect these being opened. Alternative detection versions respond to breaking glass, impact or vibration so can be fitted on frames or panels. Nevertheless all these devices always offer protection to what we know as the building perimeter or fabric of the home.

Space protection is offered by detectors that are placed in areas such as rooms or passageways. These respond to the presence of human beings. The most common detectors are ceiling corner mounted passive infra-red (PIR) sensors which detect human radiation levels which is the heat generated by the human body.

Dual technology detectors are also used in homes but these are rather more specialist as they are installed in difficult areas of the home where pulsating heat sources could cause a PIR to cause a false alarm, such as in conservatories.

CONTROL EQUIPMENT

As its name suggests this equipment controls and manages the system by turning it on and off so as to arm the premises and make it secure. The present trend is to use small compact aesthetically pleasing remote keypads that allow a system user to have their own personal code for arming and disarming. A variety of electronic keypads are available for this purpose with a range of options featuring different zone setting programmes for the homeowner. Control equipment using simple keys is now rarely used. Setting fobs may be contained in some systems.

Intruder alarm keypad. The keypad illustrates the system setting being carried out by entering a user code. The level of protection required, i.e. the zones to be turned on, is then selected by using specific keys.

Let us have a look at these three main elements, beginning with detection devices.

Detection devices are placed around or within the house to be protected. In order to determine exactly how they are to be used, the premises must first theoretically be divided into zones or areas. For instance, the external front and back doors of the house, together with the living rooms, kitchen, garage and main bedroom and other bedrooms could all be placed on separate zones and given circuit numbers. The external front and back doors could be protected by perimeter detection devices, whilst the other areas would be covered by space protection.

Specific zones can then be turned on or off at any particular point in time. Therefore, during the night, the external doors, the living rooms, kitchen and garage could all be protected, i.e. the detection devices turned on, but the

HOME PREMISES PROTECTION CHART

Circuit/zone detection type	Area	Setting A	Setting B	Setting C	Setting D
1 Perimeter	External front door	✓	✓	✓	
2 Perimeter	External back door	✓	✓	✓	
3 Space	Living rooms	✓	✓	✓	
4 Space	Kitchen	✓	✓	✓	
5 Space	Garage	✓	✓	✓	✓
6 Space	Main bedroom	✓			
7 Space	Secondary bedrooms	✓		✓	

homeowner would have unlimited access to the bedrooms, so these zones would be turned off. This is carried out by the control equipment.

All keypads provide a system user with the benefits of different setting means and a selection of protection levels. An example of turning a system on and off (arming and disarming) by using a personal code is illustrated.

If we now refer to the home premises protection chart, it gives us an example of how the house can be programmed in a variety of ways at the different times of the day or night. The system will automatically select (turn on) the circuit/zones detection devices identified with a tick [✔]. These would have been pre-programmed to allow easy system setting.

For instance, if setting A was selected, then the system would be armed with every detector selected and show Armed Away All Secure.

If setting D was selected, then the system could show Garage Only Secure. This option would typically allow a homeowner to have the garage protected during the day but give access to all other areas of the house.

Settings B or C could be used during the night-time, depending on which bedrooms needed to be protected and those that needed to be switched off for use by the occupants. Tables are always a good way of showing home-protection charts and allowing us to select our settings.

This brings us on to the subject of signalling devices.

It follows that a great many options are available for notifying an alarm condition. Indeed, progression under the European Standards places greater emphasis on remote signalling, as there is now a wide range of equipment that allows alarm signals to be received by system users or key-holders to their landlines, PCs or even mobile phones. In

SIGNALLING DEVICES

If a detection device was to be activated by an intruder when the intruder alarm system was in the 'on' or set condition then the control equipment would generate an alarm condition and trigger the signalling devices. These are referred to as warning devices (WD) in the European Standards (EN 50131) as they give notification of an alarm event.

The signalling generated by the control equipment would be:

Audible by means of internal or external sounders that can be heard.

Visual by means of beacons or strobes that flash and can be seen.

Remote by signalling over the telephone or other transmission network to a manned security centre, alarm receiving centre (ARC) or to a key-holder, a PC or a telephone.

Signalling options. In practice the signalling can range from a warning device (WD) fitted at a high elevation on a house, to the visual image of an intrusion sent for viewing on a mobile phone.

Contact switches and PIR detection devices. Intruder alarms installed in homes typically use surface (far left of picture) and/or flush contact switches (centre of picture) as perimeter detection devices. These are fitted as pairs with one device on the opener (such as the door) and the other device on the frame. Ceiling-height PIRs (far right of picture) are used to give space protection and are normally found in a corner position of a protected room or area such as a passageway.

fact, visual images of the scene are available by using intruder alarm systems linked to cameras to verify that an intrusion has actually taken place.

We are now able to appreciate that an intruder alarm is made up of detection devices placed in or around a home, which are connected to an item of control equipment that will send an alarm signal or a form of notification if an intrusion occurs when the system is 'set' or turned on.

Remember that detection devices offer perimeter or space protection, and that space detection is of vital importance to protect volumetric areas of the home.

The signalling or notification can be a basic audible sound or it may be a beacon or strobe indicator to give a visual warning effect. As an extension on the signalling, notification can additionally be sent to a remote point or to an advanced communication device or phone to provide an image of the scene when it is integrated with cameras.

So what we now need to know is how we can determine what detection devices should be installed and how many. But we also need to know what control equipment to use and also what signalling to employ.

To do this first requires that we prepare a design proposal.

Preparing a Design Proposal

In order to prepare the design proposal, the first stage is to carry out a home risk assessment using the ABC of risk as explained in Chapter 1 and to record the findings. This then enables us to select a security grade for the house according to the European Standards EN 50131, which replaces the original British Standard BS 4737. However, it must be clearly understood that, in the vast majority of cases, for domestic premises the grade established will be Grade 2, as only particularly vulnerable residential properties with extremely high-value goods and special needs would be of a higher risk grade and require bespoke systems. There is a lower grade, namely Grade 1, that may be used for some low-risk DIY projects. Therefore the grades we are interested in are:

- Grade 1 – low risk. Intruders are expected to have little knowledge of intruder alarm systems and be restricted to a limited range of easily available tools. Essentially DIY market.
- Grade 2 – low to medium risk. Intruders are expected to have a limited knowledge of intruder alarm systems and use a general range of tools and portable instruments. Essentially residential properties.

A subdivision of Grade 2, referred to as Grade 2x, is accepted in the UK for non-communicating systems, i.e. those that only have 'local' audible or visual signalling and are not connected to a remote communicating device. Grade 2x is the most common intruder alarm system type for UK homes.

Having recorded the findings of the home risk assessment and determined the risks, we are then in a position to use a chart for guidance. The table below contains the main requirements for the installation of an intruder alarm into any domestic premises, up to and including Grade 2 or Grade 2x.

As we have now reached the stage where we can plan the installation, we should look just a little further into the role that the detection devices, control equipment and the signalling devices play.

Having done that, we will then be able to look at a design specification as a conclusion to this section. This is illustrated in the table and applies to the installation of an intruder alarm system in a typical home.

Planning the Installation

Detection Devices

It remains to say that there can be no definitive answer as to the number of detection devices to be used or to their positioning – no two premises are identical. A logical approach based on the probability of intrusion at any particular point must be made with the minimum requirements from the chart as a guide. A number of PIRs to give space protection are always needed as a support for the perimeter devices. Contact switches, either surface or flush, are used on openings such as doors or windows to give perimeter protection. Glass break detectors and vibration sensors may also be used on windows and panels to offer perimeter detection.

The ubiquitous PIR detector, which is used in high volume in the domestic environment, varies enormously in terms of performance, depending on the specific version employed. In the main they are found at ceiling height in a corner of a room. Other versions may be found mounted centrally on a ceiling and offer 360-degree coverage.

Special PIRs are also available for those who wish to avoid alarms being generated by pets moving into protected areas. These are called pet-tolerant and do not respond to the body mass of dogs and cats. Therefore they can be used in those homes where the homeowner

---

GUIDANCE CHART FOR PROTECTION OF A DOMESTIC PREMISES

	Requirements (minimum)
Detection devices	Perimeter protection for all external doors and for vulnerable openings and panels. Also for windows of low security.
	Contact switches are the most common detection device for perimeter protection.
	Space protection for vulnerable areas and passageways, rooms with high-value goods (main bedroom) and outbuildings or garages.
	PIR sensors are the most common detection device for space protection.
Control equipment	A remote keypad to suit the system user, with real English text or LED display.
	Confirm outputs and approval for any particular remote communications if this is also to be a requirement.
Signalling devices	Installation of an audible external warning device with an integrated standby battery (SAB/SCB) facility. Access to this device must be difficult under normal circumstances, so should be fitted at a high elevation.
	Installation of an audible internal warning device.

does not want to restrict the movement of pets into protected areas with the intruder alarm turned on.

In every instance, the manufacturers' installation data for all products have to be taken into account.

Control Equipment

This is the heart of the system, allowing management of the system and so must suit the needs of the user in terms of the keypad display and attributes. It will enable the system to be pre-programmed specific to the protected home. It also sets the entry end exit times to allow an authorized user time to enter and exit the home through a permitted route, such as a front door, to turn off the system.

The main unit of the control equipment is often called an end station and should be installed at a secure location in the home out of sight, whilst the setting keypad should be at a point that is easy to use but is still protected. In practice the control equipment manages a multitude of intruder alarm parameters and signalling 'shut-off' times in the event that an alarm is generated. It also allows personal attack (PA) buttons to be programmed within a system to act as emergency push units and hence signal an alarm. These PAs tend to be sited adjacent to the front door (at switch height) and in the main bedroom (at bed-head height). PAs with dual buttons can be installed to stop user error causing false alarms, as both buttons need to be pushed simultaneously by means of two different fingers, which makes accidental operation difficult.

Many domestic keypads, which are used to set and unset and for control of the intruder alarm system, have built-in PA buttons so that the alarm condition can also be generated by the user direct from the keypad.

Signalling Devices

External sounders with LED indicators and integrated visual beacons or strobes are a visible deterrent and confirm that an investment has been made in an intruder alarm system.

GUIDE TO DESIGN SPECIFICATION

Design Specification – Intruder Alarm System

Three-bedroom, two-storey home with an attached garage and utility room.

Security grade 2x.

Address

Detection Devices

Surface or flush contacts installed on the external front door, external back door and patio door to provide perimeter protection. Surface contact installed on the utility room single-glazed, wooden-frame window to provide perimeter protection.

PIR detectors installed in the lounge, dining room, ground-floor passageway, first-floor landing, main bedroom and garage to provide space protection.

PA button installed in the main bedroom.

Control Equipment

A remote keypad installed in the ground-floor passageway close to the front door. This door wlll be the system final entry and exit point.

System parameters to be programmed to suit the system user.

Exit and entry times to the premises to be set at 30 seconds.

Signalling Devices

An audible external warning device with an integrated standby battery and complete with a beacon/strobe installed at first-floor height on the front of the premises.

An audible internal warning device installed in the ground-floor passageway.

A decoy/dummy warning device installed at the rear of the premises at first-floor height for its deterrent effect.

Notes

Other forms of system signalling to remote points, using more specialist techniques, can also be used but these form a wide subject, so we cover these in their own right in Chapter 6.

To complete this section let us take as an example a cost-effective but secure design specification for a popular semi-detached home with an attached garage using only local (audible) and visual signalling.

At the end of the design specification we can include notes of any special requirements. These could include details of the use of any pet-tolerant or special dual technology detectors. The notes can also state the way in which the programming of circuits/zones could be planned to allow them to be turned on and off for the different setting times that will be used throughout the day and night.

Although intruder alarms have always formed the nucleus of the electronic security systems industry there are other techniques also used to great effect.

Next we will look at methods used to verify access to the home and by callers to the premises.

INTERCOMS, DOOR ENTRY AND CALL SYSTEMS

Historically, intercoms, door entry and call systems have been known to us as access control systems. In fact they are all electronic security systems that exist as a means of attracting someone's attention in order to gain access, or admittance, to domestic premises, or they may be used to seek assistance. In all cases they provide a reliable method of restricting access to the home so that only authorized persons may gain entry to the house.

Alternatively, they may be used so that the occupant of the home can check the identity of a caller before opening an entry door, or they may be employed to make a call to a further area of a house or, remotely, to a monitoring point.

Although we have classed them as of three different identities, in practice they may overlap or be interlinked to share facilities. However, in order to see what they offer we will overview the application of the three different techniques on an individual basis.

INTERCOMS

These comprise a call station which includes a speaker and is connected to a telephone within the house. The call station is mounted in a position such as next to an external door. A button that is incorporated on the call station can be pressed by a caller which causes a buzzer on the home telephone to sound. This enables the caller to speak to the homeowner via the telephone and to prove their identity.

DOOR ENTRY

Door entry systems are based on intercoms but they tend to also have a keypad reader on the call station which allows an authorized person to enter a code or PIN into the keypad.

Certain other forms of verification for more diverse applications are available such as card, token, tag or physical attribute.

A valid transaction, when entered at the keypad, enables the door to automatically unlock.

CALL SYSTEMS

These are used to provide a call for assistance, confirm that a call was received and ensure that the person making the call receives a visit. They use a unit of dialling equipment or a control panel to which are connected call devices such as push buttons or pull cords. These push buttons or pull cords may be linked to the dialling equipment or control panel by wiring or by using a wirefree transmission such as radio.

When these call devices are activated the control panel sends a signal to a further part of the house or to a monitoring station over the landline telephone or mobile network.

System Security Guide

So, with some knowledge of the function of intercoms, door entry and call systems, we can now give an overview of some popular system configurations and how they may be specified in terms of security features. Although there is an enormous range of options available, leading to customized systems and an overlap of application functions, the table below can be used as a typical system guide for selection purposes.

Security and Safety Aspects Guide

All intercom, door entry and call systems provide unique security functions and can be customized, interlinked and adapted to suit any specific needs. However, there are certain considerations to be taken into account for all these systems to ensure that the maximum benefits are gained from them. This is particularly evident as they are electrically powered.

GUIDE TO INTERCOMS, DOOR ENTRY AND CALL SYSTEMS

Requirements	Security features	Considerations
Intercom	Allows the homeowner an opportunity to check the credentials of a caller from the security of any number of rooms within the home. Systems use audio speech methods. Equipment that also provides a video image of the caller is readily available.	These are ideal systems for controlling access through external entry doors. Multiple doors can be controlled. Additional telephones can be employed in a number of rooms. Extensive operating distances between the call station and telephones are possible. Can be installed to replace door bells with little difficulty.
Door entry	Allows access to the home by authorized persons entering a verification code or PIN into a keypad reader. Other methods of identification are possible, such as using a card, token, tag or physical (biometric) trait.	Enables authorized persons to have credentials that give them ease of access to a home. Keypads can be electrically powered or they may be mechanical versions. Allows system operation by multi-users without a need for a large number of keys to be cut.
Call systems	Enables calls for assistance to be made easily. Call devices, such as push buttons or cords, can be fixed or carried by a system user. Bespoke systems can hold operational data to confirm a call was made and then acted upon by means of a reset function.	Control equipment can be linked to a remote monitoring station or generate a local audible sound to seek assistance. May be used in neighbourhood watch schemes or form part of a larger or local authority network. They are often linked with intercoms.

System Backup

Some thought has to be given to system backup in the event that the main electrical supply could be disconnected. In most domestic environments the actual probability of disconnection of the main supply is low. However, for areas where security needs are high, provision should be made to install a power supply unit (PSU) with standby rechargeable batteries.

These standby supplies allow the system components to work from the main supply under normal circumstances, but in the event that the normal main supply is lost, they then work from the integral standby rechargeable batteries located in the PSU unit.

Door Security and Strength

Since many security systems also incorporate electrically released doors, these do need to have electrical locks installed on them. It is important to ensure that the strength of a door, when installing an electric lock, is never compromised. In other words, make sure that the door strength and its locking potential is not lowered by electrifying a lock.

Be aware of all of the regulations that may apply at the time for the type of home you live in.

Remember also that in every instance, once an electrical lock has been installed, there is a need for mechanical key backup and emergency manual overrides. It is not the case that doors can be electrically automated without the need for mechanical devices able to override the electrical function.

Although electronic and electrical components are inherently reliable, it is still possible, in the worst case scenario, they may become defective.

Emergency Exiting

For those points that may include emergency exiting, such as in communal home complexes and apartments and flats, note that emergency exit doors must be easy to see, easy to open with one simple motion only, have minimal hardware and not be locked from the inside.

BS EN 179 and BS EN 1125 relate to emergency and panic exit hardware.

The Security Selection Process Guide

For all of these technologies there are a number of things that we need to consider within the selection process.

Intercoms

It was the increasing use of apartment-type housing developments and gated communities in town centres, with restricted access through communal areas, that lead to a greater use of intercoms. It was also this awareness that promoted the advantages they offered as security systems for any home, no matter how small.

Apartment-type housing developments always have intercoms installed at the source of their building development to provide communication between remote entry doors and specific apartment rooms. These are governed by the building maintenance and community agreements. In all cases they incorporate push buttons on the telephone to unlock the main entry doors to authorized

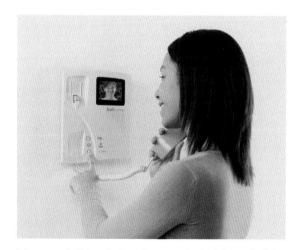

Intercom unit. This unit allows the owner to check the credentials of a caller, who is outside the premises, from the security of any number of rooms within the home. This particular system features an audio-speech method, plus a video image of the caller.

callers, so as to enable them to enter the main building concourse.

All homes may have intercoms installed to aid their security, no matter their size or type of architectural construction. They can replace the normal door bell push and have a facility to automatically open a door (normally an external door) by means of a button on the telephone to which the outside call station is connected. Extra telephones can be added within the home so that the external door can be interrogated from any number of points and these extra telephones also have the ability to allow talk between each other.

Kits with specific connection information and installation data are available to the homeowner or installer.

Units that provide video images for improved security, and that can record images of the caller using particular observation systems, are becoming increasingly popular.

Door Entry

This form of electronic security system when used for the home mainly uses keypad readers that have a code or PIN entered into them. This method of identification allows a door to be unlocked by an entrant to the premises without the need for a mechanical key. It provides a secure locking facility for users without any need to generally issue user keys. Only an emergency key needs to be held in the event of an electrical fault. Such systems allow codes or PINs to be changed on a scheduled rotation basis to aid security.

There are actually three recognized methods of identification used in door entry access control namely:

- **Knowledge.** This is the most popular type used in the residential sector and is derived from a code or PIN being entered into a keypad reader.
- **Possession**. This is based on the holding of a card, token or tag, which holds data within its construction. These are presented to a reader. They may be non-contact, i.e. the card, token or tag can be presented to the reader from a specific distance, so does not need to be placed against the reader. These non-contact systems may also be used to open barriers and gates from cars.
- **Personal characteristic.** These are known as biometric systems as they verify the unique personal features of the person trying to gain entry. They include fingerprint and eye iris recognition.

The variety of keypads and options is enormous. They range from budget low-cost units with

Door entry keypads. The most popular form of door entry for the home is the electronic keypad reader to which a code or PIN can be entered. This operation permits entry through a locked door. An enormous range of devices are available for the home.

very basic functions, through to vandal-resistant devices that are capable of being installed in difficult outside environments.

The most popular keypads are electronic because this enables them to carry out electrical functions; however, locks fitted with mechanical tumbler keypads are also available.

Knowledge is the most generally used method of identification used for the home. As a guide we can look at the merits of the coded keypad.

The only security issues with all electronic keypad readers follow the use of all PIN protection in that the user needs to be vigilant in not allowing the code to be viewed by others. For security, and if it is suspected that unauthorized persons have viewed the code, it can easily be changed. Indeed it is wise to change the code periodically in any event.

It is fair to say that door entry systems and intercoms, alongside call systems, may actually be found as fully integrated systems; in other words they may all be interconnected and use

purpose-designed control equipment to also include intruder alarm technologies. However, in order to best understand their individual identities and unique roles, they need to be studied separately.

We will look at call systems next.

Call Systems

These allow calls for assistance to be made easily. Therefore this technology is more related to the security of the individual, rather than to that of the premises in which it is sited or from where it is controlled.

Call buttons. The radio push call button can be moved around the premises to suit the user.

GUIDE TO CODED KEYPADS

Compact
Easily meet the aesthetics of any home. Robust and provides good weather protection.

Facility to Change Codes
Different codes can easily be programmed for improved security and change of users.

Maintenance
Servicing and maintenance is not difficult.

Inexpensive
Easily replaced or repaired with no complex hardware.

Nothing to Lose or Forget
There is nothing to carry or misplace. This is an advantage over using cards, tags or tokens, etc.

Understandable
The general public are now familiar with the use of codes and PINs.

In their most basic form they comprise control equipment that will generate an alarm, either audible or over the telephone network, to a designated point. In the more advanced network they can form part of a local authority or government network or scheme. In all cases they should be able to confirm a call was made and then acted upon by means of a reset function.

Call devices, such as push buttons or cords, are used to generate the call for help. Although these can be fixed in position, it is normal to use radio-frequency units that can be carried around the house or worn by the user. These are generally worn around the neck and are known as pendants. The range in which these are capable of operating varies, but it tends to be up to a distance of 100m. We can see these portable devices, which in this case have small red operating buttons, moved to different parts in a home setting.

Intercoms, door entry and call systems are all often used with techniques to allow doors, barriers or other openings to be automated, so these can be opened from remote points. It is these methods that we turn our attention to next.

AUTOMATED OPENING METHODS

We always have the facility to electrically control doors, i.e. to enable them to either lock or unlock electrically from a remote point. This can be an aid to security, as it allows the homeowner the facility to control the locking feature of the door from a secure position.

However, before electrifying any lock, ensure that the security of it cannot be compromised by installing a mechanical door-closer to ensure that the door is physically returned to its closed position where it may then be held by the lock. These door-closers are easily fitted and have adjustments to ensure that the door can close easily without clashing.

Although this need applies to doors, a much more complex system is required for any home that has external gates or barriers that require automation for safety reasons. This is to meet legislation and safety requirements to ensure that gates cannot trap or collide with persons or vehicles, and to confirm that the route of the gate is kept clear of obstructions. These safety systems will be supplied purpose-developed for the automatic closing equipment being used.

In practice, almost any gate or barrier may be automated, so that any existing gates, etc., which were originally purpose-made, can be upgraded.

Swinging and sliding gates tend to be the most popular for the home, as rising bollards and rising arm barriers are mostly used in commercial areas.

Having automated gates allowing access to the home, rather than gates that must be manually opened and closed, is not only very convenient but security is enhanced because:

- **The gates become monitored**. The position of the gates is checked by the system, so they cannot be left open. If they have been left open, a warning signal can be sent to the house.
- **Callers enter into a controlled environment.** Persons and vehicles, once they have been given permission to enter the grounds of the house, are effectively in a held position. Callers know that their exit from the grounds of the house has been blocked and that leaving the area without permission will be difficult.
- **Automated gates have a deterrent effect.** To the observer, the use of automatic gates states that the homeowner is prepared to invest in positive security measures. It suggests that the other issues of security for the home have also most likely been upgraded.
- **The automation can be recorded**. The operation of the gates can be recorded for time and attendance. The homeowner can hold a computer database for the operation of the gates so that callers are recorded on

the system. This applies when regular callers are given an entry tag, code, etc. Being remote, it can be read by the gate controller to allow cars to enter through the gates.

Automated doors and barriers can also be linked to other systems so that images of callers using these facilities are monitored visually. The subject of viewing these pictures is considered in the next section. Indeed, it is in the monitoring of areas around the home using cameras that major developments are taking place.

CCTV AND OBSERVATION SYSTEMS

Closed circuit television systems (CCTV) have come to play an increasingly large role in the home security sector and are used to great effect to monitor or watch particularly vulnerable areas around the perimeter of a house or an area within it or close to it.

We use both the terms CCTV and observation systems as the methods or techniques by which we can capture and view the images from cameras. These images are viewed on monitors in a similar way to which we can see images on a TV screen. Although we use the terms CCTV and observation systems interchangeably, in practice, observation systems tend to be rather smaller systems. Indeed, for homes it is observation systems that probably present the best opportunities.

Rules and Regulations

With the widespread use and development of CCTV as a security aid for the home, numerous rules and regulations were drawn up. A significant piece of legislation is the Data Protection Act (DPA), which affects anyone who installs, owns or uses CCTV equipment. The only exemptions are domestic users who install the equipment to safeguard their homes.

The Act was supplemented by a Code of Practice issued by the Information

CCTV monitoring. Small CCTV or observation system monitors can blend into any home environment. They can be used to watch the live images or views from an individual camera or from a number of different cameras. These images can also be recorded and 'played back' later, if required.

Commissioner's Office. This, in conjunction with the DPA, was intended to ensure that CCTV systems were installed and used responsibly without impinging on the civil liberties of individuals. From this it follows that providing a responsible use of CCTV is made in terms of safeguarding our homes, then there can be no objection to its use. In fact, due to the small amount of restrictions on its use, and its value as a security system, it subsequently developed very quickly in the domestic market. This led to the manufacture of widespread unobtrusive and modern components for the CCTV home market, which can easily blend into any domestic environment.

A Guide to System Selection

The Code of Practice suggests that those who are considering having CCTV fitted should initially carry out an assessment to confirm that it has an important role to play and that its objectives cannot be achieved by any other

GUIDE TO CCTV AND MONITORING SYSTEM SELECTION

Basic System Viewing Activities

Use a wired or wireless camera kit. These come as a kit that is 'plug and play', i.e. a kit containing all of the parts that enable them to be easily connected direct into the existing TV in the home.

The camera may send an image by connecting wires (wired) or by a method not needing cables (wireless). These kits are very cheap but they are only capable of being used to view live images, i.e. as they occur from the camera/s, so they do not have any method of recording the activities that have been viewed.

Basic System Viewing and Recording Activities

Use a wired or wireless recording camera kit. These are similar to the previous system but they include a digital video recorder (DVR), so the activities that have been viewed can also be recorded and 'played back' using a home TV. The DVR has a special channel for each camera connected on the system. These kits are relatively cheap and are easily fitted.

Viewing and Recording Activities on a Specific Monitor

Use an observation system, which comes as a kit containing all of the required parts to make up a system for both viewing and recording of activities. These systems also have a monitor so viewing can be performed at the most convenient point, rather than having to be carried out on the home TV. They are competitive in price and are largely governed by the number of cameras they can control and the amount of recording of CCTV footage they can store but they cannot normally be extended.

Observation systems are ideal for those homes wanting a clearly defined operating system at a realistic cost; they are easily fitted.

Custom-Designed CCTV Systems

Use a system comprising purpose-specific parts, each of which is specifically selected to suit the application. They present the most successful solution and are capable of carrying out a multitude of functions, but need to be professionally installed.

Note: IP (internet protocol) cameras are programmed and connected direct into PC systems as against using DVR recording facilities.

measures, such as improved lighting or an alternative security system.

The use of CCTV as a security method is extremely wide and can be used in a range of applications, but for the home it is mainly used for monitoring and/or recording events around the perimeter and grounds.

Having decided that CCTV is the optimum method of security system required for the application, the design must:

- Avoid any unnecessary invasion of personal privacy. The siting of cameras and their views must be carefully controlled. The owner of the system is legally responsible for the management, operation and control of the system.
- Not capture images outside the 'protected area'. Taking images of people in adjacent buildings or not visiting the protected area must be avoided. The owner of the system is legally responsible for control of the recorded material or 'data' produced by the system.
- Provide images of sufficiently high quality. The cameras should be installed so that the captured images are of adequate resolution for identification purposes. We use the term resolution as a means of expressing how well the system is able to 'resolve' or show fine detail in the captured images. Resolution means the ability to resolve detail; so by using high-resolution cameras and monitor screens we get better images for viewing.

When designing or selecting a system we need first to gather our thoughts and decide what we are trying to achieve by taking a budget into account.

The main issues are:

- What do we want to be able to see on the monitors and where should we locate the monitors?
- Do we want to be able to record the images for storage and playback at a later time?

A huge amount of options are available to us with CCTV to cover these issues. This means that an affordable system is possible for any home and, although we have an overlap in terms of these systems and their components, if we refer to the guide, we can see what we need to consider.

Kits are ideal for the home: they include all of the required components, they clearly define how the system will operate and the homeowner knows that all of the individual parts are compatible with each other and will form an effective system. The custom-designed systems are much more involved than kits but do produce an optimum operating system, as they use specially selected components. However, they must be professionally installed to get the full benefit from them.

Any CCTV or observation system requires a camera and lens. Having decided on the target area to be viewed, we can then think about the camera and lens.

Camera and Lens

Monochrome (black and white) cameras are superior to colour cameras in low lighting environments but colour cameras are better for identifying targets during the day. For this reason many cameras now automatically switch from colour during the day, to black and white at night.

Dome cameras are normally used for homes as they are aesthetically pleasing and it is not possible for the observer to know what they are looking at. For other applications, small bullet cameras can be hidden.

In all cases select a camera that has protection from the weather, particularly if they are exposed to the elements.

The human eye has an angle of view in the order of 35 degrees and it is this same angle that a normal or standard lens will see. So if you want to know exactly what image will appear on your monitor, if you are using a standard lens, then all you need do is place your head at the position that the camera is to be installed at.

A 'wide-angle' lens would be able to see a larger scene; in other words it would be able to see a greater and wider area, but all of the objects in the scene would be smaller. A 'narrow-angle' lens would make all of the objects in the scene larger but the area viewed on the monitor would only be small. Therefore it is practice for mainstream home applications to use a normal or standard lens, as it will correlate to the normal field of view of a human being that we are used to.

If you want to improve the security of the camera, it is possible to use a further camera and use it solely to watch the main camera. In this case a criminal must attack them both simultaneously, which is rather difficult to do.

Recording and Viewing Equipment

The digital video recorder (DVR) is used to store (record) the CCTV images digitally on to a built-in hard drive from a given number of cameras. These multiple pictures can be shown on a traditional CRT monitor or flat screen of any size. The images can be displayed individually or using a multi-display on the monitor so that all the camera pictures appear simultaneously; or the DVR can be connected into a PC network for viewing over the internet.

As an example, 'quad' displays, as the name suggests, show four cameras simultaneously on the monitor, whereas other multi-displays can show considerably more camera images by splitting the screen into further appropriate-size portions.

More advanced options take us to the connection of the system into laptop computers and mobile phone or pocket PC devices for viewing and control purposes.

In fact it was the rapidly developing commercial CCTV market and its use in places open to the public that drove the introduction of budget systems for the home, to the extent that even domestic systems can come complete with a sophisticated range of features.

So security for the home can now benefit from such things as fully functional cameras that can automatically move to cover various scenes and zoom in to capture specific details. They may also operate in the dark using LED illuminators without a need to provide any other artificial lighting. This of course all goes alongside the already mentioned options for viewing the images that are available to us.

However, we should never lose sight of the basics of adopting CCTV for home security by considering such things as:

- **Protecting the camera.** Cameras need to be installed where they are not easily accessible to vandals and criminals, but they also need to be protected from the weather. Select cameras that are both robust and weatherproof.
- **Protecting the DVR and its data**. The DVR should be installed in a secure location together with the data that may have been taken from it. It is important to ensure that a DVR is selected that will give the correct amount of storage (recording), so that the system can be managed efficiently. This storage information can be obtained from the manufacturer.
- **Protecting the image from the camera.** In order to be alerted to the loss of any images from the camera, it is advisable to use a DVR that provides an audible response if any image is no longer being received from the camera. If images are not being received at the DVR, then there can be no recording of any events!
- **Checking the available lighting.** Cameras cannot see in the dark but some cameras are better than others in low light conditions. Make sure lighting is available for night-time use. An option is to use cameras that have infra-red lighting in the form of LED arrays, as these enable the camera to see in the dark without any further lighting having to be installed.

What has to be stressed with CCTV and observation systems is that we have a vast range of options with something to suit every home's budget.

Criminals and intruders do not want to be recorded on camera. Even those who use masks to conceal their identity know that their general physique, responses and physical movements can be something of a giveaway when caught on good recorded material. This is much more apparent when these recordings are shown to persons who know or are familiar with the criminal.

Even though the images alone may not be sufficient to prove an individual is culpable, they often guide the police towards the criminal with a view to investigating them further and to look for other forms of additional evidence.

We will now look at a rather different security-related subject covering the detection of fire and carbon monoxide.

FIRE AND CARBON MONOXIDE DETECTION

Smoke Alarms

The security and the protection of property from the devastation of smoke and fire are helped by the installation of smoke alarms. In point of fact this is all endorsed within the Regulatory Reform (Fire Safety) Order that applies to England and Wales (Northern Ireland and Scotland have their own regulations). This Order covers general fire and other fire-safety duties that are needed to protect persons in case of fire in and around most premises, including the home. The Order requires fire precautions to be put in place where necessary and to the extent that it is reasonable and practicable in the circumstances of the case. Responsibility for complying rests with someone who must be designated as the 'responsible person'.

The Fire Safety Order uses a fire-risk assessment approach, which asks that an assessment be made to prevent any fire from occurring by removing or reducing hazards or risks, and then looking at the precautions to ensure that persons are adequately protected if fire were to occur. The fire-risk assessment must also take into account the effect the fire may have in or around the premises.

The fire alarm should provide adequate warning that automatic fire detection is provided where necessary and that the system is being maintained to highlight significant, unwanted alarm issues.

Although different needs apply to different dwellings, it is the single family dwelling home that we are interested in. For this the requirements are:

- **New dwelling**. Smoke alarms must be mains-operated, have false-alarm control with at least one fitted on each storey in circulation routes within 3m of bedrooms and 7.5m of other rooms. Smoke alarms should be interconnected so that any smoke alarm going into an alarm condition will also generate an alarm at all of the other smoke alarms in the home.
- **Non-new dwelling**. Battery-operated smoke alarms may be suitable if they are fitted in similar areas to those specified for new dwellings. These are known as Grade F systems and have 9V batteries. These are easy to install because they are self-contained and do not need any electrical connections.

Although all smoke detectors have to be installed by competent persons, this is most apparent for those that are mains-operated, as against those that only have 9V batteries for their electrical supply. For the larger system it is also the case that the installer and the person commissioning and checking the system should be different people. This allows a further perspective to be placed on the credibility of the system, on the basis of an input coming from two different sources.

In terms of selection, optical smoke alarms are the preferred choice to detect smouldering fires and to avoid nuisance alarms from cooking. They should be installed in circulation areas, such as hallways and stairways, and where furniture fires may be detected. For this reason we always find them at the stairways and landings because it is at the highest point that the smoke will concentrate. Therefore, as a minimum always install them at the top and bottom of the stairs for houses and in the passageways of bungalows.

It is only for large, stately homes that we may now see fire-alarm systems with control and indicating equipment (CIE) or a control panel that identifies the exact location of any detector that has gone into alarm. These are now only used for the commercial market.

Carbon Monoxide Alarms

Carbon monoxide (CO) is a highly poisonous gas produced when a fossil fuel, such as gas, coal or oil, etc., burns incompletely. Being colourless and having no taste it is difficult to detect.

The sources of carbon monoxide are:

- Blocked and cracked chimneys.
- Blocked flues or corroded flues/vents.
- Badly installed and maintained combustion gas and solid fuel appliances.
- Back-drafting through chimneys and flues.
- Appliances without flues.
- Exhaust fumes from cars run in garages.
- Gas cookers, grills and boiler and water heaters.

Protection can be helped by fitting carbon monoxide 'kitemarked' BS EN 50291 detectors in the home corresponding to any of these area hazards. These will provide a warning signal when they detect levels of CO, long before they reach harmful levels. This means that, even if fuel-burning appliances are regularly serviced, protection is given in the event that a problem has occurred between services.

Combination smoke and CO alarms (sometimes referred to as 2-in-1) are available and give different warnings when either smoke or CO is detected. As a security supplement to smoke and carbon monoxide alarms it is also worth considering having a small, home fire-extinguisher in the hallway that is easily accessible from most areas of the home.

BATTERY-OPERATED SECURITY SYSTEMS (WIRELESS)

Special smoke and carbon monoxide alarms can often be linked with other electronic security systems to give us what are called integrated systems. These provide enormous benefits in terms of overall security because they bring together a number of different security aspects. However, what may concern the homeowner is the need to run cables within the house in order to have any system installed. This means that the homeowner may be reluctant to opt for larger or extended systems. A good option is to consider what are known to us as wireless systems. Of course wireless technology has been making great advances for many years – we only need to look at mobile phones to prove this. These wireless security systems use components known as transmitters and receivers to carry their signals so there are no wires, mess or fuss. The lack of cables makes installation simple and quick, and there is no need to remove carpets or lift floorboards, and so on. Such systems are also fully supervised so that the strength of the signals is continuously checked.

For those homeowners who want to have any electronic security installed but are concerned about wiring, there is the option of a wireless system. Today's radio-based wireless systems are a world apart from the early days of wireless system. New-generation wireless systems are very reliable and suitable for genuine security applications, and are also available to the professional installation market. Batteries have also changed enormously, so they can give a longer life to support wireless components. Wireless systems offer new technologies and a range of benefits not available before to the upper end of the installation sector. They are

also recognized by the European Standards, so do not need to be seen as inferior to those hard-wired systems that have all of their components connected to each other by wires and cables.

It is worth noting that hybrid systems are also generally available. These are effectively systems that have options on wiring or being wireless. In other words those parts of the system that are easy to run cables to are fitted as such by using wires. For those areas where this is difficult, then this is accommodated by using wireless techniques via radio transmitters and receivers.

So with hybrid systems we can use either, or a mix of, the two different methods. These options ensure that we do not need to compromise on security for those home applications when cabling may be an issue. This applies to any type of electronic security system, as they are all now have wireless versions, no matter what type of security role they offer.

Although the competent practical home owner is capable of fitting certain security systems to their own home, and in particular wireless equipment, it is sometimes the case that there is a need to use professional industry services. Also, for some homes the insurance company that underwrites the policy for the home may insist that an approved installation company is used to fit certain security systems. We cover this in the next section. However, first let us mention the most asked questions of wireless security systems:

Q. Are they difficult to install?

No, because radio signals are used for the system devices to communicate with each other.

Q. Is there any disruption?

There is very little disruption because there is no need to run cables throughout the house.

Q. How long do the batteries last?

Battery technology is now very good, so lifespan is not a serious issue. The control equipment can also notify of 'low battery', so that the system is not compromised.

Q. How do they compare with systems that have wires?

In terms of standards, methods of use and features they compare well with wired systems.

Q. How do they compare in terms of cost?

The components used in wireless systems in relative terms are more expensive to buy than wired systems, but savings are made in the system installation costs.

Q. Can the owner take them away if moving house?

Yes, it is possible.

SECURITY SYSTEMS: ACCREDITATION AND MAINTENANCE

Under the Association of Chief Police Officers (ACPO) Security Systems Policy, those installers that fit automatic police-calling intruder alarm systems need to be approved by recognized inspectorates that are accredited by the United Kingdom Accreditation Service (UKAS). Therefore, if an alarm system is to be installed to generate an automatic electronic call for help to the police through an alarm receiving centre (ARC), the installer of that alarm must be approved by a recognized inspectorate. This means that the homeowner must have their security system fitted by a company that is approved by either NSI or SSAIB, if they are to have an automatic police response. However, the police have priorities, and any response or attendance by the police will still be subject to the priorities they have at the time.

If an intruder alarm system is installed by a non-approved company, it does not mean that the police will not attend, it just means that the alarm cannot be automatically generated to them in an electronic way. Nevertheless it could still be relayed to them via a personal call to the control-room.

Of course using an NSI- or SSAIB-approved installer illustrates a professional installation by a company that is prepared to invest in being accredited through an official industry route. The insurance company will always confirm the status required for any intruder alarm system subject to how they view the home risk. It should be noted that non-approved NSI or SSAIB company installations may well still be acceptable to the insurer if they work to the required standards and use local signalling or signalling to a neighbourhood watch scheme.

All electronic security systems are sensitive, so do need regular maintenance. This is called preventative maintenance. This maintenance is a condition of NSI and SSAIB installers but in fact servicing does need to be carried out for all security systems. Intruder alarms should be serviced once per annum if they have local audible signalling only, whereas those that include remote signalling are normally subject to maintenance twice per annum. In fact some forms of maintenance can actually be carried out by the installers from a remote point using diagnostic equipment without a need to visit the home.

BEWARE

Preventative maintenance may be invoked within the official national or European standards or industry specifications, which govern all of the security systems installed in the home. If maintenance was subsequently not carried out, this could be in breach of the insurers' stipulations for the home cover. This can be even more critical for fire detection using smoke alarms.

---

chapter five

Lighting for Security

It is rather difficult to define lighting that is to be used for home security purposes. This is because it can be found in diverse forms across a range of applications and includes large variations in levels of illumination. In fact any lighting does provide an element of security, even though it may be quite marginal.

Statistics do show us that intruders and unauthorized or unwelcome persons are intimidated by light because it can make them more visible to the casual observer who may report their presence. Equally, good street-lighting schemes have long been proved to give good protection against the threat of robbery and muggings.

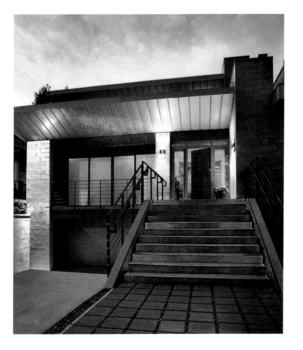

So with all of that in mind, what can we say is the object of lighting for security purposes, and how can we select the best system?

Well, first of all think of how insecure and unsafe our home would be if it was in total darkness and there was no lighting whatsoever in the surrounding area. This would be similar to a power cut in the area with a total blackout occurring. Now consider if we added even a very small amount of light in the area. Our home would then, in relative terms, appear much more secure and safe, despite only a small measure of illumination being available. Therefore, it follows that a large measure of security and safety is achieved, even if only a small level of light is added. For this reason any lighting does provide an element of security, no matter how marginal that light may be. Nevertheless we may always want to add further lighting to a particularly vulnerable point of the home to heighten the security of it and because we want that point to be better lit for general amenity purposes.

So we are about to look at how the introduction of lighting will improve our home security and general safety. Initially we will study how external lighting can be applied for security purposes for the outside of the house, before also looking at some internal lighting schemes. In fact we can immediately see how much value, in terms of security, can be added to a house if we refer to the illustrations.

Approach home lighting.

Rear home lighting.

The lighting at the approach to the house provides a very good measure of security and amenity by giving a reassuring glow around the perimeter of the premises. It is not overpowering, so is not expensive to run. Equally, it does not create any light pollution because the lighting is controlled within the environment it is intended to serve.

The rear of any home is generally more vulnerable. It can be noted at the rear of the home that the level of lighting is essentially the same as for the approach to the house. Notice also that multiple lights are used.

It is better to use more but less powerful lamps, than to use fewer brighter lamps, as this is a more secure method of countering bulb failure. Certainly it is apparent that if only a single lamp was installed, and it was to fail, and no other local lighting was available, then this would create a total black-out.

So let us now consider how we go about selecting our external lighting.

SELECTION OF EXTERNAL LIGHTING

The three main reasons for employing external lighting to enhance our security are:

- It deters crime by providing illumination in a given area.
- It heightens the security and safety of authorized persons in the area in which it operates.
- It supports the operation of other security techniques.

Lighting actually falls into two broad categories, namely: extended period lighting and demand lighting.

Extended period lighting is energized for long periods of time such as from dusk to dawn. It is therefore available whenever natural light is unavailable and gives a reassuring presence to the homeowner. In addition, intruders and unauthorized persons are always reluctant to enter into an area where lighting is already available because they know that they are entering into an area in which they will become immediately visible. Therefore it has a high deterrent effect and is a truly effective security method. Extended period lighting is the general, time-honoured type of lighting that we are all familiar with.

Demand lighting is rather different. It is activated by automatic detection devices that make the lighting only available for a short period of time and on demand. We will look at this later in the chapter.

We may want to protect different areas with different levels of risk to security. For example, the front door to a home, which is visible to many homeowners of adjoining houses, would be basic security with amenity, whereas a vulnerable patio door at the rear of the premises could either be mid or high risk. The box below indicates the general type of extended period lighting we can employ.

Notice we tend to use the word luminaire, as this is now widely used as a generic term for an actual light fitting.

In some cases homeowners like to use low-level lighting, i.e. lighting that is installed at ground level or close to the bottom of walls. These lighting systems make use of 'brick lights' or 'deck lights' or 'louvre lights'. They are good for safety purposes as they light pathways very effectively but the luminaires are, of course, easier for a criminal or vandal to attack. If the security risk is not high, these lights can be an option, provided that robust versions are used which offer high resistance to impact.

Timers and photocells (dusk/dawn sensors) are popular devices that switch lights on and off automatically. This brings us on to the subject of automatic lighting systems in which these devices have a major role to play.

AUTOMATIC LIGHTING SYSTEMS

In these days of automation, when many of the tasks we wish to carry out can be performed in an automatic way without a manual operation being required, we find that this also applies within security lighting schemes.

Timers and Photocells

The most important components in automatic lighting systems are timers and photocells. By using these devices it means that the homeowner does not need to remember to switch the external lighting on during the hours of darkness, since it will be done automatically. This, of course, heightens security by taking the emphasis off the homeowner to have to carry out a routine task. Equally, the lights are turned off automatically, so no energy is wasted.

Timers can be easily protected from vandals since they may be mounted inside the home at a secure point. They can also include a number of different options and a range of programmable setting times.

Photocells need to be installed on the outside of the home. This is because they must be sited in a position from which they can measure the available natural light. Therefore, they must be fitted at a high position close to the roof.

Both timers and photocells can be fitted with an override. This means that the lighting could, if ever wanted, be energized outside the normal selected automatic periods by means of an override switch. This is a benefit to security because, if a fault was to occur with the timer

---

GUIDE TO THE SELECTION OF EXTENDED PERIOD EXTERNAL LIGHTING

Basic Security with Amenity
Almost any standard luminaire or decorative fitting will provide a measure of security and amenity by providing a reassuring glow around the perimeter of the home. Use low-energy bulbs rather than low-wattage old-style bulbs.

Mid Risk
Use luminaires that cannot easily be damaged by vandals, such as bulkhead fittings where the bulb is enclosed. Avoid decorative fittings that have the bulb exposed and are fitted at a low height. Use timers or photocells to control the lights automatically, so that it is not possible for the homeowner to forget to turn them on at night.

High Risk
All luminaires must be difficult to gain access to, so should be at a high location. Timers and photocells must also not be capable of being reached or attacked. Cables should not be visible. Use discharge lighting floodlights. Employ more luminaires so that the bulb failure of any individual unit is supported by the installation of additional luminaires.

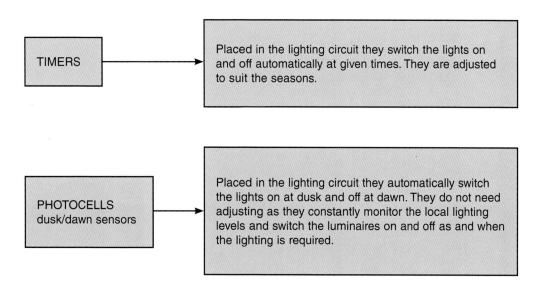

| TIMERS | Placed in the lighting circuit they switch the lights on and off automatically at given times. They are adjusted to suit the seasons. |

| PHOTOCELLS dusk/dawn sensors | Placed in the lighting circuit they automatically switch the lights on at dusk and off at dawn. They do not need adjusting as they constantly monitor the local lighting levels and switch the luminaires on and off as and when the lighting is required. |

or photocell, it means that the lighting could at least still be turned on manually.

DEMAND LIGHTING SYSTEMS

Demand lighting, as the name suggests, is only illuminated on demand and for short periods of time; which can even be as short as a few seconds.

A huge variety of detection devices are available to activate the lighting, which can then be kept illuminated for a set period of time. In fact the lighting can be activated by any electronic security sensing device, including invisible active infra-red beams (IR) placed across an opening or gate, or even activated by sensors placed under the road or driveway. However, the most popular device for home installation is the external passive infra-red (PIR) sensor. For many years these have been used in high volume in the home market. They represent excellent value for money, are inherently reliable and weatherproof, and understandable, so overall they form the best option for activating most forms of residential demand lighting.

These PIR sensors can be found 'built-in' to a diverse range of luminaires, so a choice

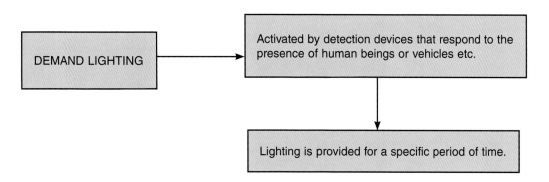

| DEMAND LIGHTING | Activated by detection devices that respond to the presence of human beings or vehicles etc. |

Lighting is provided for a specific period of time.

of lighting is available for low-risk security applications. In other words the PIR sensor and the luminaire are one combined unit. The PIR sensor itself only needs to be checked for its detection pattern to confirm its suitability for the proposed area. Allied to this of course, the luminaire needs to be able to produce a respectable lighting level for the area to be protected.

For higher risk areas it is advisable to use separate luminaires and sensors. By doing so the luminaire can be placed at its optimum position and so can the PIR sensor. This is a better option because both the PIR and the luminaire can be installed at their most effective position, rather than compromising security by having to fit both of them at the exact same location. It also means they can both be installed at more suitable secure positions.

A useful option is to use a demand lighting system that allows a push button to be sited in the house close to the external door. This push button does manually what a movement sensor would do automatically. In other words, if the push button is pressed, the lights will immediately come on and stay on for a selected period of time; hence we have instant light. Therefore, if the homeowner is leaving the house, they do not have to take a number of steps outside the premises in order to activate the sensor but they have light available before they even leave the home simply by pressing the push button. This is both a security and safety aid.

Since demand lighting is only intended to operate for short periods of time, it must use luminaires that give instant light. Historically it has been used with old-style filament bulbs or tungsten halogen floodlights (tubular or bulb projector), but due to the high energy consumption of these light forms they are losing popularity and so are no longer the normal choice.

Tungsten halogen floodlights can now only have a role to play in high-security applications when mounted at a high position. Although

they give instant light, they have high power consumption and their bright white light effect can disturb neighbours. Also, they are easily damaged if impacted. If they are to be used for a specific high-risk application, ensure they are projected downwards to avoid lighting other areas outside of the intended points and that they are in a location that makes them difficult to impact. If tungsten halogen floodlights are already installed, the user can change the bulbs for energy-saving halogen lamps to go some way towards making cost savings.

As it happens, due to developments with energy saver (low-energy) light bulbs and their ability to light up straight away, there is no reason why these new-generation bulbs cannot now be the light form for most mainstream demand lighting systems, including within floodlight housings.

The truth of the matter is that modern energy-efficient light bulbs have evolved to the extent of providing fast warm-up, long life and both energy and financial savings. We also have a progression towards floodlights that use electronic bulbs, known as light-emitting diodes (LEDs), or make use of solar energy. These can all be used with confidence.

LED lighting is very energy efficient. In effect it is a more specialized form of low-energy lighting using electronics technology, which is becoming increasingly popular, as it is incredibly reliable and has a long lifespan.

Low-Energy Lighting

In these days when everything seems to be judged for energy efficiency, low-energy lighting is becoming the dominant force, including its use in security lighting schemes. Indeed, the Building Regulations have always specified that a given number of fittings must be energy efficient and as time has progressed, the number of fittings that must meet this requirement has been increased in percentage terms within these Regulations. Therefore, the security requirements for the home have also had adapt to support such changes.

Low-energy light bulbs do take a little more time to warm up before becoming as bright as a regular traditional bulb (known as incandescent or filament bulbs) but in real terms they do still light up quickly enough. In addition they last longer than traditional bulbs, so are more reliable and offer greater security than old-style bulbs. They also have lower wattages because they use less energy, not because they are necessarily less bright.

The main forms of discharge lighting are as follows:

- **Low-pressure sodium (SOX).** These have high efficiency, so are the dominant source used in street-lighting schemes. They provide a monochromatic light of an orange/yellow form.
- **High-pressure sodium (SON).** They provide monochromatic light of an orange tinge form and are effective when used alongside CCTV systems
- **Metal halide.** These provide a clear, white light, so are good for security but can be a problem if light pollution in the area may be an objection.
- **Mercury.** These have a cool, white light and are an alternative option to metal halide.

An important thing to consider when using discharge lighting is light pollution, as the creation of high levels of illumination can be a nuisance to neighbours. White light, such as emitted by metal halide and mercury lamps, is very good for security but does clearly contribute the most to light pollution. On balance, high-pressure sodium is the optimum light form taking everything into account and should be the first considered for home high-security risks.

GUIDE TO THE SELECTION OF LOW-ENERGY LIGHTING

Basic Security with Amenity
Low-energy bulbs have been developed to directly interchange with regular bulbs and should now be the preferred choice, since they can be used in almost any enclosure that was originally intended for regular bulbs. Compact fluorescent lamps (CFL) are a variant low-energy bulb fitting and come complete in an enclosure and can be used with confidence.

Mid Risk
Mainstream low-energy bulbs and compact fluorescent bulbs and fittings are acceptable but some thought needs to be given to protect the luminaire from attack. Use robust enclosures and fit out of normal reach. Posts or columns can be used with the cables installed within them so they are not accessible.

High Risk
Luminaires need to be fitted at a high location and be capable of illuminating large areas. For these risks it is normal to use what is called discharge lighting, as these luminaires provide increased levels of lighting at reasonable running costs. Discharge lighting is fine for houses when it is installed at roof level but it is not recommended for bungalows as the lamps can run hot and users may approach close to a strong light source. For bungalows it is advisable to use posts or columns with the cables installed within them so they are not accessible. The main types of discharge lighting are low-pressure sodium, high-pressure sodium, metal halide and mercury lamps.

Low energy and traditional regular bulbs. Low-energy bulbs (two bulbs to left of picture) are available in a variety of sizes and fittings to replace the regular traditional bulb (right of picture). These low-energy bulbs improve security due to their increased reliability and lifespan.

INTERNAL LIGHTING SCHEMES

In theory any existing lights in a house can be altered to come on automatically in order for the premises to look occupied, even though no one is actually at home. I say in theory because in practice it is rather more complicated to add devices to existing lighting wiring circuits.

If a house is being newly built or refurbished it is rather easy to put in custom circuits and devices so that internal lights can be controlled automatically to a given sequence, in order to improve security; this suggests that there are always persons in the house during the hours of darkness. With such systems it is possible to use the general internal amenity lighting but to add to it an automatic role with customized control equipment. This adds an option to the internal home lighting that complements the normal switching on and off carried out using standard manual switches. It also enables the luminaires in the house to be used to great effect, as no additional lights need to be purchased.

In general, external lighting is always more easy to add to a home because cabling is not as difficult to run as that for internal lighting schemes, especially when homes are fully decorated.

There are switches that are available to replace existing internal light switches. These have automatic settings for light control but the fitting of these devices needs to be checked professionally to ensure they can retrofit the original switches and not cause faults with the existing wiring. For this reason, for internal lighting schemes it is advisable to use 'stand-alone plug-in' solutions to improve security, unless as stated, the home is being newly built, refurbished or professional advice is available for a specific existing lighting application.

So, on the basis of the foregoing, for those homes that are fully decorated and are looking for a good solution for internal lighting schemes it is to best to use a number of plug-in devices with timers that are programmable and capable of switching lamps on to random sequences.

Selecting internal lighting schemes.

These plug-in timers are simply plugged into a standard socket outlet, which in turn controls standing lamps. Therefore, the plug-in timer acts as an interface between the socket outlet and the standing lamp. Low-energy bulbs can be used, so these home security methods are not expensive to maintain.

Using a number of devices enables them to be programmed so that as one light goes off another comes on. This gives the impression to the casual observer that someone is present and moving around the house, and turning lights on and off as they do so.

A further type of device is what is called the night light or photocell light. These turn themselves on when the normal lighting in a particular area drops quite low, so that illumination is then always present. Such night lights also plug into standard socket outlets and may be self-contained in that they actually feature a bulb or they may allow standing lights to be plugged into them. Either way, as with all internal lighting security schemes they provide a measure of protection by suggesting that there is presence in the home during the hours of darkness.

A good place to use any of these variant devices is in the hallway and at the top of staircases, as this allows light to be dispersed throughout the home, especially if internal doors are left open.

Historically homeowners have often used internal lighting schemes in conjunction with leaving a TV or radio playing in the background to give the impression that the home remains occupied. For those who subscribe to this logic of using multiple devices and feel comfortable carrying this out, it continues to have distinct merits. Obviously the only disadvantage lies in the cost of the use of additional electrical energy.

The best means of selecting your internal lighting scheme is to try to visualize the layout of the house with no roof on. It is normal to regard the hall as the focal or starting point and then to do a risk assessment to decide which areas are best illuminated for the times when natural light is unavailable. This will give you a chance to decide which areas could have light applied, how light could be generated around the premises and how lighting could be switched on and off in sequence. This can all be done in conjunction with the planned use of TVs or radios or any other devices that could give the impression to an outsider that there was presence in the house at different periods of time.

SELECTION OF LUMINAIRES

Before selecting luminaires there is something we must first understand: all luminaires are rated in watts. This is the power that the lamp uses. Therefore, this rating in watts relates directly to the cost of running the lamp, so the higher the watts quoted, the greater the cost of running the light. This is important, especially when luminaires are going to be switched on for long periods of time. However, different luminaires use different ways of producing light, so it is not exactly true that the higher the rating in watts, the more light will be available for our security purposes. For instance, when we compare low-energy bulbs and regular traditional bulbs we will find that approximately an 11-watt, low-energy bulb produces an equivalent amount of light to a 60-watt regular traditional bulb. Similar comparisons can be made for other low-energy and regular traditional bulbs for the other available ratings and equivalent amounts of light output.

The low-energy bulb is more expensive to purchase initially but in the long term it has clear benefits in terms of economy, being favoured due to its greater life and increased reliability, down-time and robust construction. Therefore it has distinct benefits for our home security needs.

GUIDE TO EXTERNAL LIGHTING

Protection
This is to be considered against the weather and also against attacks on the luminaire by vandals. Filament bulbs, which include incandescent bulbs and tungsten halogen lamps, are easily damaged by impact. Try also to bury power lines and protect switch boxes for all lighting systems.

Shadows
These are caused if luminaires are badly sited and have an obstruction, such as a wall, fence or tree, in their path that creates a barrier to the light being projected, so always locate perimeter lighting to allow illumination on both sides of any barrier. Shadows allow intruders to hide. Design lighting to permit overlapping illumination for different lighted areas.

Glare
This occurs if the homeowner or an authorized person walks directly towards a strong light source. It is normally associated with the lamp being fitted too low and not being angled correctly towards the area it is intended to illuminate, so always make sure that the directed light does not hinder observation. This is a common symptom of badly installed tungsten halogen floodlights at low heights.

Delay of Lighting
If discharge lighting is used there is a dwell time for the lighting to come on. This type of lighting is not intended to be turned on and off periodically but is to be left on for extended periods.

Access to the Luminaire
The more difficult we make the luminaires for criminals or vandals to reach, the more difficult it also becomes for the authorized owner to get access to them, so use high poles when practical. Consider also the changing of bulbs and maintenance.

Remember that compact fluorescent lights are a well-established and further version of energy-saving bulbs. They are ideal for home external and internal lighting since they last up to 15,000 hours and save approximately 80% of energy compared to regular incandescent bulbs. These compact fluorescent lamps come in a range of sizes and enclosures, so can be used with confidence for home security lighting up to mid risk.

For security purposes there are a number of other things we need to think about. In particular, for external lighting luminaires we must consider certain issues because external lamps are always going to be more vulnerable and subject to greater abuse than internal lighting components.

When selecting your luminaires for outside duty for the home, never flood large surrounding areas with high-wattage, harsh, white, bright light to the extent that it can interfere with neighbours. It also creates light pollution, so has to be limited. Give a measure of thought to the environment and always try to use low-energy lighting or discharge lighting, such as SON, and keep it in controlled areas specific to where it is actually required. Lighting also uses main voltages, so the greater number of luminaires, the greater is the need to satisfy electrical safety requirements.

As we know, luminaires can be controlled in many different ways but don't overlook how they can be used with simple switches to protect walkways and dark passages around the outside of the home and garden. For instance, if a homeowner needs to walk down a dark passageway, this can easily be served by two manual switches, with one switch installed at each end of the passageway. The first switch turns the lighting on as the passageway is entered, the other switch turns it off as you leave the passageway at the far end. This is simple, gives good security and is cost-effective. The switches only need to be protected against the weather.

If CCTV is to be used at night, use cameras that can work at lower light levels or use infra-red illumination. This infra-red illumination is invisible to the human eye so does not cause any light pollution. However, it is visible to a camera lens and as we actually see on a CCTV monitor, what the camera sees, then no other visible lighting is needed. Special infra-red luminaires are installed to match the camera lens or the camera comes equipped with its own infra-red arrays to enable it to work in complete darkness.

For external lighting schemes we have noticed that the selection of luminaires can be rather complex, as we move between the levels

Controlled lighting for a staircase with a particular security need. The lighting is directed on to that area using a number of durable low-energy LED lamps. These give off an energy-efficient, cool, white light to highlight the staircase. Being capable of offering directed light, they cannot cause light pollution or irritate neighbours, and they clearly offer the staircase a good level of security.

of risk. For internal lighting the considerations are rather less complex, since we do not really need to consider an attack on the luminaire or difficulties with the environment in which they are sited.

Avoid using old-style, regular traditional bulbs as these all use filaments to produce the light source. Filaments easily damage and often snap when the lighting is first turned on because they heat up very quickly. This can, in some cases, cause the local lighting to trip out due to a quick imbalance in the lighting circuit, which of itself can generate a security problem for the home.

CONCLUDING THOUGHTS

Lighting has a high-profile role to play in security and is an excellent security tool. A burglar would prefer to use a torch with a very much more directed beam of light to carry out an intrusion, rather than work in general lighting. This all endorses the high status of lighting for security.

Since lighting, by its very nature, exists in every home for general amenity, we should always look at ways to use that which is already available to us to help improve our overall security or to adapt it accordingly. Also, try to integrate the lighting with our other security systems, so that it can be brought on if one of the other systems is activated.

Nevertheless we need to accept that lighting, by its very nature, cannot give us twenty-four-hour protection because its use is limited during the daytime when natural light is available.

Think also of using low-energy and new-generation lighting systems, as old-style traditional bulbs convert only about 5 per cent of the electricity they use into visible light.

It is also important to use more, but less bright, luminaires, rather than use a lesser amount of more powerful units, as this caters better for lamp failure. Equally, try to use different circuits for the different luminaires used specifically for large security areas whenever possible. This helps to overcome circuit failure problems that may close down large critical areas rather than only closing down smaller parts of them.

chapter six

System Signalling and Self-Contained Security Devices

In this chapter we are going to look at how we apply the signalling from the security systems that we use. We will also consider the role of key-holders who we have elected to care for our home and how a response can be made in the event that alarm signalling is made to these parties. Home automation in terms of its security duty is then mentioned. To conclude this chapter we will show how small, miscellaneous devices can be applied at very little expense to provide us with an alarm system signal and to contribute an element of security, no matter how small it may be.

In order to put security in place, or to draw attention to ourselves or the premises in which we live, it is often the case that we need to use some form of signalling or notification. In other words, if we want to seek assistance or wish to bring attention to an area, we often must apply some type of warning so that the criminal realizes that either they have been detected committing an offence or we are in the process of summoning assistance.

The word notification is often used because this term has been adopted in the European Standards to show how signalling is carried out and in what form it exists, namely:

- Audible – the signalling can be heard – typically sounders.

- Visual – the signalling can be seen – typically strobes or beacons.
- Remote – the signalling is sent to a monitoring point or station – uses telephone networks or free space transmission.

LOCAL SIGNALLING AND NOTIFICATION

In practice, audible and visual are known to us as local signalling, even though they may be signals that are heard or seen at a considerable distance from where they are actually generated. For example, an audible signal or sound generated by an alarm installed at a house and subsequently heard at the far end of a housing estate would still fall under the category of local signalling despite the long distance from its source. Equally a strobe seen flashing at the same point would also be classed as providing local signalling.

Audible Signalling

Audible signalling is generated by sounders, speakers or similar devices that generate a sound or level of frequency. Under the European Standards they are referred to as warning devices (WD).

GUIDE TO SOUND AND SOUNDERS

Sound loudness follows a logarithmic scale, so does not have a linear effect. Therefore, do not install multiple sounders in the belief that in doing so, a large increase in sound can be achieved. Increasing the number of similar sounders in an installation will only give you a very limited increase in sound.

External Sounders

When selecting an external sounder for an electronic security system, use a device that is being used in the mainstream industry. This means it will be EN 50131–4 compliant, be of the required frequency, not conflict with the frequencies used by the emergency services, be enclosed and weatherproof, have the correct mean sound level and be self-powered in the event its supply is disconnected by criminals and will not draw too much electrical power from the system. They also shut-off after a particular time interval and normally also have a visual strobe feature.

Compatibility

Use a sounder compatible with the control equipment it is connected to. Avoid the use of bells or mechanical sounders for the home installation. Electronic sounders are more reliable.

Installation

Install external sounders as inaccessibly as is possible and ensure that they are fixed on a solid structure. Keep the sounder free from high, dense hedges or trees, or these will reduce the effect of its sound.

Internal Sounders

Be careful when selecting internal sounders for homes that share dividing walls with other houses.
Note: Low-frequency sounders, i.e. those with a bass-type effect, have a long wavelength so also have an increased ability for their sound to penetrate all type walls, which can be an irritation to the homeowners of adjoining properties.

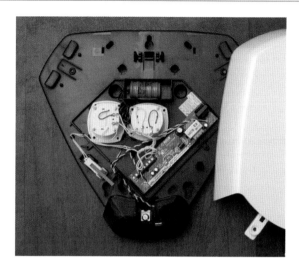

This external sounder includes a strobe that is mounted at the bottom of the unit and is protected behind a small, blue, translucent screen. Always select an external sounder that is EN 50131–4 compliant, so it will not conflict with the sound frequencies used by the emergency services. It will also have the correct mean sound level, together with an inbuilt sound shut-off and will normally include a strobe to give a visual warning signal.

Noise is defined as unwanted sound; therefore, sounders, or warning devices, to the letter of the law do not produce noise but they do generate sound or audible signals. However, if the sounder becomes a nuisance, it could be blamed for producing noise. That understood, we have available to us an enormous range of sounders to choose from.

Always select an external sounder that is used as a mainstream device (see box opposite).

Let us now give some thought to the application of visual signalling.

Visual Signalling

This is a type of signalling that can be seen by the human eye and tends to be used as an additional and inbuilt feature of most self-contained external sounders. The specific devices that carry out this function are known as xenon strobes or beacons, which produce a brilliant flash of light. This signal from high-power visual signalling devices can be seen at a distance of several kilometres, depending on the background illumination.

External sounders with built-in visual signalling are fully weatherproof, so can be installed in positions that are exposed to the weather. Although visual signalling can be used on its own, it does, in the main, tend to be used alongside audible signalling.

There are a number of advantages to the use of visual signalling:

- It shows specifically the area from which the alarm is being generated.
- Although audible external sounders need to silence after a maximum period of twenty minutes, the visual signalling device can continue for an extended period of time.
- Using different colours of signalling can signify what type of alarm has occurred, i.e. red for fire and blue for intrusion detection.

REMOTE SIGNALLING AND VERIFICATION

Remote signalling is carried out by a transmission signal that is sent to a monitoring point or station from the protected home. This signalling can be by the use of telephone networks or it can be by free space transmission, such as radio, which do not involve any wiring, in much the same way as a mobile phone works. Such a monitoring point or station can be as simple as that of a friend's house used to help out under a neighbourhood watch scheme. Otherwise it can be as involved and well-organized as an accredited alarm receiving centre (ARC), which also carries out a vast range of services in the monitoring of alarms and other communication signalling for commerce and industry.

Advances in technology mean that security systems can now make greater use of remote signalling to a larger or lesser degree. They can transmit signals using a number of different formats and can also connect to a PC based at a remote engineering centre or alarm receiving centre equipped with specific software to upload or download system parameters, including the event log and diagnostics. It could also set and unset the security system

and carry out additional special functions. They may also send live video images from CCTV and observation systems, over the internet, to an individual's PC, laptop computer or even to their mobile phone anywhere in the developed world, using specific client software.

Other options exist, such as when an alarm event is triggered, a motion detector or even a door bell in the system can be configured to send a series of emails from the communication equipment to a chosen email address. These can have JPEG attachments to show the activated CCTV camera image taken before, during and just after the alarm occurs. This is known as electronic mapping, in that events can be sent electronically in a visual form to the new-generation range of mobile phones, as well as all of the other modern communication and IT devices in the home sector.

We even have talkback that enables a warning or announcement to be made back to the area in which the alarm event was triggered. This informs an intruder, who has entered an area, that they have been detected and their activities are being processed.

So, remote signalling and verification often involves the capture of images relating to a person. What must be understood when becoming involved with the use of CCTV images is that care must be taken over their use and disclosure. Remember that the Human Rights Act 1998 takes precedence over the Data Protection Act, so if someone feels that CCTV has infringed their personal rights, they could bring an action citing Article 8. This deals with 'The right to respect for private and family life, home and correspondence'. The Regulation of Investigatory Powers Act 2000 (RIPA) legislates to protect people from danger, whilst safeguarding their privacy. Furthermore, the Freedom of Information Act 2000 applies to requests for CCTV images made to the public authorities.

BS 8418 applies to the installation and remote monitoring of detector-activated CCTV systems and sets out guidelines and recommendations for their design, installation and operation to

Remote observation by laptop computer. Video images can be viewed anywhere in the developed world using laptop computers. They enable areas of the home, such as the front drive and approach road, to be watched live or played back to check how the status of the area may have changed over a period of time.

enhance their performance.

The other governing document is BS EN 50132–7, the European-harmonized standard, which includes further guidance on the design implementation of CCTV. If automatic police response is required, then accreditation by compliance with BS 8418 and the European standard is needed.

It is interesting that CCTV is making enormous strides in the development of sending live or recorded remote images to new-generation technology equipment but it is becoming allied to an array of complex rules and regulations if images are not to be taken outside the controlled bounds of the law.

Modern technology enables remote observation of events to be viewed on laptop computers anywhere in the developed world. Events can be as basic as watching the drive to

a home or replaying footage to see the changes in the status of the drive over a period of time.

However, for the more standard home installation requiring audio messages only, an electronic security system can send a very basic, automatically created voice message to a neighbour's home via a speech dialler in order to alert the neighbour to an activity. Otherwise it can send an SMS text message to mobile phones.

In fact it is the speech dialler that has the most prominent use within the mainstream home installation market for remote signalling and alarm verification. Also known as voice diallers, or in some cases auto-diallers, they are available in various forms. They simply plug in to a standard telephone outlet point and are programmed to provide a voice message to a number of call recipients in relation to the security system to which they have been connected. Inexpensive and easily connected, they represent true value for money as they provide a simple message or messages for different security systems. They are not highly secure, since they do not have to be connected to a monitored line in the house, but they are extremely reliable and capable of dialling both landlines and mobile phones.

The guide provided explains what is needed for the system signalling for a domestic intruder alarm security system and is a benchmark followed by the professional installer. However, for those who wish to have automatic police response (we cover this in the next section), you will find the installer has to be approved, able to issue unique reference numbers (URNs) and needs to include monitoring equipment to provide secure remote signalling. A variety of methods are available to do this with secure communications. Dual communications are used by professional approved installers for high security risks, using both landline and mobile networks, so that the communications support each other.

We are now going to overview the architecture of security signalling within the industry that is available to us.

GUIDE TO THE SELECTION OF HOME SECURITY SYSTEM SIGNALLING

External
An industry EN 50131–4 compliant external sounder (warning device) with a strobe to give a visual warning signal mounted at high elevation or somewhere difficult to get access to under normal circumstances.

Internal
A small, electronic sounder mounted at ceiling height in the home. An extension speaker to provide entry/exit and system fault tones close to the final exit/entry points.

Remote Signalling
A speech dialler to dial a given number of key-holders and to relay a voice message advising of the type of security system alarm-activation.

Note: A decoy/dummy alarm box installed at high elevation is also recommended.

SECURITY SIGNALLING RISK

To satisfy a low to medium level of security risk applicable to a residential property:

- Employ signalling as on left (*see* box).

For higher risks and automatic police response it is necessary to:

- Use a professional industry-approved installer who can issue URNs. This can include the use of CCTV images for remote monitoring.

Security Signalling – a Guide

For automatic police response it is necessary that an intruder alarm system, which we recognize as the nucleus of electronic security systems, must be fitted by an approved installer. In these cases the alarm receiving centre (ARC) will receive the alarm signal transmission and then relay the information to the police in order for them to attend the home, albeit subject to police response priorities. However, there must be verification because all this takes up police resources, so 'confirmed activations' must be made. In other words, the alarm system must be installed to meet certain criteria to ensure that false alarms are avoided.

Confirmed activations can be achieved in a number of ways; the principal means are:

- **Audio.** Following an alarm-activation, the ARC actually listens in to the home to ascertain whether or not the alarm is genuine.

- **Visual.** The ARC operator analyses recorded images from the house to ascertain whether or not the alarm is genuine.
- **Sequential.** This is a technique by which detection devices in the house are set up to prove that someone is actually moving around different areas of the home and that the alarm has not been generated as a result of one individual detector generating an alarm signal.

Although the ARC will receive alarm signals and provide response services whilst carrying out monitoring for homes and commercial and industrial practices alike, they will also act as key-holders for those homeowners who wish to subscribe. However, it is not only just the ARC who is capable of carrying out key-holding and providing a response. We will look at this next.

KEY-HOLDERS AND OBTAINING A RESPONSE

Key-Holders

Key-holders provide a service for the homeowner by holding keys to the premises. This enables the key-holder to enter the home to check and confirm that there are no problems in the house when the owners are not available. It also allows the key-holder to check any alarm-activation that may have occurred with the security system and to reset the system, as required.

The key-holder may be a relative, friend or member of a neighbourhood watch scheme. On the other hand, the key-holder could be an official security company responsible for monitoring the security systems, such as the intruder alarm, that the home may have installed.

Key-holders are of particular significance for those properties that are in settings with no near neighbours because those homes need to have remote communications in order to obtain a response if there is an alarm-activation.

Audible signalling on its own may be of little benefit if there are no neighbours living close and there is little chance of the alarm being heard by a passer-by.

If the homeowner is away on holiday or the house is unoccupied for an extended period of time, there are certain things that any key-holder can do to give the impression that the home is not vacant. This helps to reduce the probability of it being targeted by a criminal.

As a guide and to suggest there is regular presence in the home, the following recommendations can be made:

- When visiting the home, the key-holder should vary the times of calling. This creates uncertainty in the mind of the criminal as to when visits are being made.
- Ensure no mail is left in the post-box or is visible, and no deliveries have been left on the doorstep, etc.
- If vehicles are on the drive, turn them around or alter their positions. If garden equipment is available, such as wheelbarrows, these can be moved to new positions to suggest there is regular human presence at the premises.
- Move dust-bins to a new position randomly.
- If no internal security automatic lighting is installed, it is best to leave an inside light on occasionally but to no set sequence or time.
- Open and close curtains periodically.
- Alter the position of gates from closed to open periodically.

- Mow the grass to illustrate presence around the house is available.

Obtaining a Response

Although the various types of persons or bodies operating as key-holders will willingly attend to an alarm-activation to check the home, there are rather different requirements if an automatic police response is required.

Originally, alarm systems that required an automatic police response were connected to what were known as auto-diallers. These auto-diallers would dial 999 if the alarm activated and the police would then respond. However, it is no longer acceptable to programme any automatic dialling equipment to directly telephone 999, as there must now be a person who accepts responsibility for contacting the emergency services. Also, the police will only respond to an alarm-activation depending on their priorities at the time. Of course, if a neighbour or observer was to actually witness an intrusion taking place due to having heard an alarm from any system and was to contact the police, this would be a priority for the police.

However, an alarm-activation in itself would not be a police-response priority, if there was no confirmation of it being a true alarm. This is because it could be down to a system malfunction, i.e. false alarm. So where does this leave us?

In order to qualify automatically for police response under the Association of Chief Police Officers (ACPO) and ACPOS (Scotland) policy, there is a need for the alarm to be monitored and the installers to be approved by NSI or SSAIB. For monitored intruder alarm systems, the police will only offer a response to a verified alarm system that has been granted a police unique reference number (URN) and has been routed via an alarm receiving centre (ARC) that itself has specific operational approval. Security installers covered by the NSI and SSAIB schemes comply with these requirements, so their installed systems do qualify for police URNs. In all other respects, the police will continue to respond to 999 calls, as appropriate.

Therefore, the homeowner must decide with advice from their insurance company to what extent they want a response to their alarm to be effective, taking into account their security risk and of course financial budget.

- They can rely on audible and visual local signalling being effective enough to protect their home.
- They can elect to have a professionally installed and ARC-monitored alarm fitted to qualify for automatic police response, subject to police priorities – but at least it will obtain police response.
- A compromise is to use a neighbourhood watch or key-holder scheme by employing signalling through a standard speech dialler or via digital alarm signalling equipment.

Standard equipment enables alarm transmission signalling to be made to a number of pre-programmed telephone numbers using regular telephone lines. This, of course, allows calls to be made to anyone with a landline or mobile phone.

Local security companies will, as a matter of business development, be willing to receive and collect calls from such equipment and to then send out their company manned response persons to check the state of the home. If necessary, they could then alert the police if there was an obvious and definite need.

Home automation and integrated systems can also form a part of system signalling and we look at this subject next.

HOME AUTOMATION SECURITY

Home automation does have an influence on security, so we will give it a mention for the purposes of this guide. It is a technique for automating systems within the home so that those systems will then be automatically controlled to include energy management. By these methods, a manual input by the homeowner would no longer be needed to any great extent.

Indeed, as the IT and the security systems industry evolved, and as they became integrated with each other, the home automation sector developed as a part of these. X10 evolved as the international standard for communication among electronic devices used for home automation. It is sometimes referred to as 'domotics'.

What we now find is that modern, high-end security systems do include many functions that allow them to carry out home automation tasks. These systems are often referred to as integrated systems, so in practice, home automation and integrated systems do overlap.

The main issue, particularly when a great deal of automation is required, is that the cabling must be installed at the early stages of building the house because it can be difficult to fit purpose cabling into a fully decorated and carpeted home.

Home automation in a complex form can even extend to TVs switching off if no person is in the room for a given period of time, and landing lights coming on automatically if somebody gets up during the night.

But the question to be asked is, what parts of home automation can benefit security? Actually, the answer is probably only limited by the imagination of the user, but security of itself can be helped by using a number of automated functions.

The functions we are about to mention can be pre-programmed or they can be activated from a remote point at a particular time, using the internet and purpose-designed communication equipment.

These functions would, of course, be governed by whether the house was occupied or vacant, so there would need to be times schedules allocated to them:

- Lights turned on and off.

- Curtains, blinds, gates and shutters close/lock.
- The security system automatically selects certain zones for the different times of the day.

In theory, all of the mentioned functions would benefit the overall security of the home but the complexity of the cabling for individual control can be difficult. Also, bespoke software would be needed for the individual house. Nevertheless it does give us a further indication of a future development for security for those homes that warrant such high levels of protection.

It is fair to say that some functions can be carried out by wireless formats that use radio waves to communicate with the different sensors and lights, but a certain amount of cabling is still always needed. It can also be said that mobile phone technology can be used to control the operation and sequence of automatic functions, and we expect to see this trend continue to develop.

Lighting management systems can also be integrated within the home automation concept. These incorporate sensors that detect both presence and absence, so that the lighting is controlled by the actual presence of persons in specific areas.

It was actually the awareness of global warming and the desire to improve efficiency in homes and reduce the costs for energy that made the homeowner think more about turning off appliances and reducing lighting levels when the house was vacant. To do this easily, the advantages of having control from a single point in the home became apparent.

The user can set their security system and power down all selected appliances at one control panel. This can be done as the house is being left or when going to bed at night, so there is no need to go around the premises checking all of the individual switches.

It follows that, if the security functions are automated, then they cannot be forgotten, so security is enhanced. It is also possible to install simple pass switches, so that any complex functions are easily bypassed by the employment of a manual switch to ensure system user-friendliness.

Automated gates often form a part of integrated systems and home automation (*see* top photo overleaf). These gates can be controlled from the house or from a remote point. Alternatively, they can be opened by an approaching vehicle by means of a control fob, so there is never any need to exit the car; therefore the security of the driver is enhanced.

Swing gates are in fact the most used in domestic applications. An alternative is the sliding gate, which, as its name suggests, slides rather than swinging from hinged positions. Sliding gates are incredibly strong but do tend to be more common in commercial settings.

The sharing of facilities of course means that resources are better employed and security can be heightened in those instances where responsible persons live side by side (*see* bottom photo overleaf).

Having given some thought to home automation and integrated systems, we will now look at some rather less complex and expensive security options that can benefit us all.

MISCELLANEOUS HOME SECURITY DEVICES

Often a homeowner may want to use a small, self-contained security device that will provide an alarm or some other form of signal if it detects some type of intrusion. Otherwise the homeowner may want to use some sort of inexpensive device to aid their security in some other way, such as by use of an intercom or light.

By self-contained we mean something that is stand-alone, in that it is not connected to something else.

These devices do give a level of security, although it may only be marginal. Nevertheless, in some instances, the homeowner may be very comfortable with the physical security they

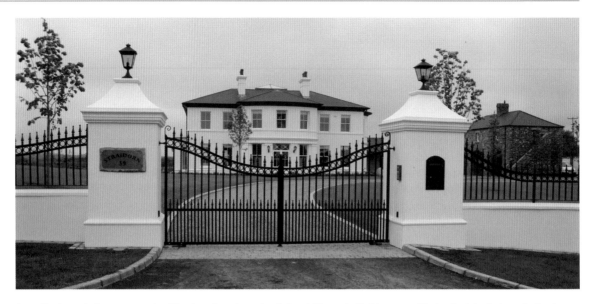

A prestige home in its own grounds with automatic swing gates that could be controlled from a multitude of points, that may be local, or perhaps from a remote area at which they could be observed and monitored. They certainly suggest to the criminal that the homeowner has invested in high security measures.

A rather different home development, which includes a number of properties in the same grounds. These all use a common automatic gating system but with a facility that they can all be managed individually.

have and feel that they only need some small electronic additional devices to raise the overall profile of the premises.

There are a number of devices on the market to which we can refer as being miscellaneous home security devices. They are battery operated or plugged into a main socket outlet,

so no complex or professional wiring is needed.

It is surprising just how many small electronic devices appear on the market and that suggest they provide security.

Patio door alarms sense if the patio door is forced open. These devices use magnetically operated sensors on the door and frame and respond if they are moved away from each other in the event the patio door is disturbed. Although often referred to as patio door alarms, they are of course not restricted to use on patio doors alone but can be used on any door or opening. They have an integrated battery and sounder for their operation. These are very easily fitted and work in rather the same way as the detectors on a shed alarm. They can be very effective in a home during the night, when the owner is asleep, because, at the very least, they can awaken the occupant and scare off any intruder who then realizes the homeowner has been alerted. They are turned off by a simple switch that is normally mounted on the device. This allows the patio door to be opened.

A variant of the patio door alarm includes a voice warning message that is relayed to an intruder. The use of a voice, rather a standard sounder, suggests to the intruder that the homeowner takes security seriously and does have a particular disturbing effect on an unauthorized person.

Patio door alarms may also be called mini-alarms or exitguards.

Shed alarms are rather similar to patio door alarms but they also include a keypad or small control panel that allows the system to be turned on and off when entry is made into the protected area. They are used to protect areas such as sheds, outbuildings and garages and have inbuilt sirens.

Keypad sensor alarms. These are a small keypad with an inbuilt motion sensor. They restrict entry past the device, which is attached to a wall or a ceiling, and are used to stop persons entering passageways or through doors, etc. The sensor is turned off either by entering a code into the keypad or by use of a remote fob. They are sometimes called occupancy detectors.

Door bell and intercom. These are wired or are cordless (have no cables) and consist of a two-piece transmitter and receiver, so the person in the house can 'screen' the visitor before opening the door. The visitor presses the button on the outside unit, which operates as a door bell. This enables a two-way conversation to be made via the intercom and allows the occupant to remain secure and safe in the home.

They may even be complete with a panic feature to alert others if a problem is encountered with an unwelcome visitor. They have an effective range quoted, which is generally in the order of 50m for cordless types. Wired types are not subject to the same restrictions on distance but sometimes the fitting of wires can be difficult in fully decorated homes.

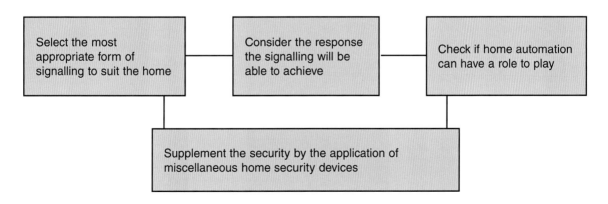

Signalling and miscellaneous home security devices.

Barking dog alarms are connected to door bells or noise-recognition modules that give the sound of a barking dog if the door bell is pressed or if a noise in the vicinity is detected. Some versions can even be adjusted to provide different types of dog barking tones.

Siren alarm padlock. A device for sheds, garages, bikes and toolboxes, etc., that operates as a padlock but gives off a short, high-volume audible sound if someone tries to tamper with the padlock. Completely weatherproof, they are robust and being made in cast steel are capable of a long working lifespan. They are available in a range of sizes and may be operated by keys or combination codes.

Motion sensor smart lights are employed to detect any movement in close proximity to the device and then turn on a super-bright white light using electronic bulbs known as LEDs. After a set period of time, they automatically turn back off. Used in dark spots around the home or perimeter, and being weatherproof, they are used to greet guests or deter intruders.

Solar lights gather solar energy during the day time, which they store in battery cells and then distribute this light at night, so they are capable of giving off a glow to act as a deterrent. Being self-contained these lamps are easily placed at appropriate positions, often in gardens or at the perimeter of the home.

DIY alarms. Totally wireless alarms come with a variety of options and intrusion sensor components for DIY installation. They may have solar external sirens with electronic lighting LED indication and be capable of sending messages over the telephone lines to remote locations and to mobile phones to include text messages. These alarms are provided with full fitting instructions for the confident DIY practitioner but include many variations on use and capability. They are, as their name clearly suggests, deliberately geared towards installation by the handyman or person, as

there is no need to run cables between the different parts of the system (being wireless) and therefore making installation easy.

Smoke/fog emission systems. These are used to fill an area with a non-toxic smoke or fog when they have been activated and can be stand-alone or be connected to wider intruder systems. The smoke or fog prevents the intruder being able to see anything in the protected area, forcing them to leave the scene. They can be used in rooms where particular valuables are kept.

Digital wireless camera and receivers. They can be used to automatically take images when wiring is difficult to install in and around the home. Such systems can be connected in to the house TV and may include the control equipment receivers to record events for later playback.

Distress alarms. These are wireless and plug into a standard telephone socket outlet. They have remote key fobs that can be carried or worn as a pendant. If activated, by pressing a button on the fob, the distress alarm can automatically dial pre-programmed numbers to summon assistance. Similar systems are referred to as social alarms.

Dummy bell boxes. These are employed as decoys to give the impression that the householder is interested in security and takes it seriously. The idea is to ensure that the criminal cannot recognize the bell box as being a dummy only. Therefore it must be representative of the genuine article.

It is possible to purchase dummy bell boxes that use internal batteries to power electronic LED indicators, which are fitted on the outside of the bell box. These indicators provide warning indication for a number of years, so these are the best option for those who are comfortable to only employ decoy boxes, as against an authentic alarm. Of course dummy boxes can also be used to complement proper boxes with them being installed on different sides of the house.

Dummy CCTV cameras. In the same way as dummy bell boxes, these are employed as decoys to give the impression that the householder takes security seriously. They do have a deterrent effect as long as they give a clear impression that they could be authentic working cameras.

Environmental sensors and alarms. These can enhance security and safety by checking the environment for the adverse effects of temperature extremes, improper humidity and water leakage. They provide an audible output to warn the householder of a problem occurring.

It remains to say that very small, inexpensive home security devices do always have a role to play. In fact we see new items continually becoming available as times change and we need to meet new challenges.

Old-style products can still work well. For instance, simple devices such as chimes on the front door can deter the new generation of 'sneak thieves'. These devices can be of benefit if the homeowner does not always want this door to be permanently locked. They emit a chime tone if the door is opened and work by having a small bell on the frame that is impacted by a striker if the door is opened. Chime facilities are actually something that is offered by most intruder alarms systems but in those cases they are electronic and are programmed to work when the external door sensor is activated.

For travellers, portable devices are available so that goods left in hotels or other homes can be protected by small stand-alone alarms and locked by purpose-designed siren padlocks. There are also travel safes for laptop computers or to hold other valuables, making pilfering from rooms more difficult, as the travel safes can be fastened to permanent fittings in the room.

In addition to the electrical security devices we have just mentioned, which give some form of signal, we should not overlook the humble mirror or mechanical digital locks that continue to have a role to play. These can often be supported by electrical security devices. For instance, an observer can generate an alarm warning or announcement by use of a bell push if they see someone in a mirror entering an unauthorized area or, if a mechanical digital lock is forced from its mounting, it can cause an audible sound.

Mirrors can be strategically placed to show a hidden area, e.g. around a corner.

Mechanical digital locks are easily installed and can be used on doors and cupboards to replace standard locks but do not need the use of a key, so there is nothing to lose or forget. They may come as a complete assembly with a handle or the handle can be installed separately.

Looking further we will see a constant supply of what may be called gizmos and novelties for security purposes. These can be covert key fob cameras that enable us to capture images unknown to others. Spy pens work in the same way. Wireless bullet cameras are easily concealed and enable an owner to capture both video images and audio evidence.

USB voice recorders allow the user to record a conversation of a caller at the door for easy playback on a PC to prove the conversation content.

The list goes on, but all gadgets do have a role to play.

Also never overlook the value of door wedges which are excellent when wedged under the inside of doors to stop them being pushed open internally. An alternative to the door wedge is the door blocker or restraint that is a form of bar which is wedged at an angle between the underside of the door handle on the inside of the door and the floor.

As a concluding thought, never underestimate the placement of warning stickers on the windows or doors of our homes, as they illustrate to the observer that the homeowner is interested in security issues and the probability is therefore high that security in some form or another is in operation. So to this end they are a deterrent.

chapter seven

Checklists and Planning for Security Issues

In this chapter we provide checklists and planning for security issues as a follow-on to information provided in the earlier chapters. We also provide a guide to household burglary measures to supplement our planning and checklist. We then show how we may plan for leaving home and going away on holiday.

Data are also included about governing regulations and other official bodies that have an influence in the home security sector, and coping with a burglary.

CHECKLIST AND PLANNING FOR HOME SECURITY

A checklist and planning guide can be used as a quick-start source of reference in order to assess your security needs (see box opposite).

Household Burglary Measures

Once you have carried out the home risk assessment, you are in a position to overview

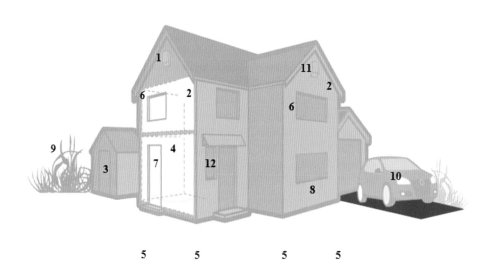

Guide to household burglary measures (see page 96). 1, alarm system bell box; 2, observation/CCTV system; 3, shed with alarm; 4, lighting timers; 5, gravel on path and driveways; 6, lighting; 7, spy hole; 8, window locks with alarm warning stickers; 9, thorny shrubs; 10, car or other vehicle keys securely locked away; 11, deterrent alarm box; 12, a safe in the house.

CHECKLIST AND PLANNING GUIDE FOR HOME SECURITY

Carry Out a Home Risk Assessment

- Record the findings.
- Give some thought to the actual premises being formed as the front, back and sides of the house.
- Have a further responsible person overview the results of the assessment.

Overview the Household Burglary Measures

- Recognize the main crime targets.
- Determine what are the 'soft targets'.

Check the Home Insurance Conditions

- Check the level of cover.
- Ensure that any special conditions are fulfilled.

Assess the Security of any Gardens, Garages and Outbuildings

- Consider the buildings, perimeter and contents.
- Give consideration to installing perimeter detection systems (PIDS).

Review Your Policy for Dealing with Bogus Callers

- Be mentally prepared to deal with callers and the need to seek confirmation of identity.
- Make provisions to cope with sneak thieves.

Check the Physical Security Measures of the Home

Review the natural and also the man-made physical restraints.
- Are trees and shrubs trimmed low below window level?
- Assess the strength of locking devices and the value of safes and visible perimeter deterrents. Doors and windows are of major importance.

Consider the Availability of any Electronic Security System

- Take account of the protection offered by intruder alarms, intercoms, door entry, CCTV and observation systems.
- Give some thought to the use of stickers on either windows or doors to state that electronic security systems are in use. An external sounder illustrates that the homeowner takes security seriously.
- If cabling the home is difficult in order to install electronic security, then consider the option of installing wireless systems.
- It may be possible to lease the system that has been selected as an option to outright purchase, which can be considered depending on the home budget.

Review Home Lighting

- Assess the external and internal lighting.
- Decide on the luminaires (fittings) to be used. Give some thought to energy management.

Consider the Options on Security Signalling for the Home

- Is the signalling to be audible (local) only or is there a need for remote communications?
- Does the electronic security need to involve installation by industry approved installers?

Confirm the Availability of Key-Holders

- Check the policies to be used by the key-holder.
- Confirm how the key-holder may respond to any security signalling.

Review the Need for the Addition of any Miscellaneous Self-Contained Devices

- Can the home benefit from any small inexpensive security devices.
- Check as to how these can be installed and if any maintenance is needed.

Check any Local Authority Terms and Conditions for Changes to the Home

- Is there a need to contact any other authorities or inspection bodies?
- Can the neighbours be affected by any extra security measures applied to the home?

Check Your Budget

Certain security issues will not involve any costs because they only involve a change in routine or maintenance of things such as hedges and shrubs, and more diligence in how we approach our security issues. However, any building work involving perimeter protection plus the installation of electronic security systems do have associated costs and maintenance requirements.

Ensure when it comes to cost that every aspect of the charges are taken into account and do not assume that everything is included in a contractor's price.

Notes

the household burglary measures. These measures will very much depend on the home type in question but we can mark up a picture or home sketch to show the measures that already exist or we intend to apply in the future.

1. Fit an alarm system bell box in a prominent position.
2. Install an observation/CCTV system.
3. Lock the shed and fit an alarm.
4. Install lighting timers.
5. Use gravel on path and driveways.
6. Install lighting.
7. Fit a spy hole.
8. Install window locks with alarm warning stickers.
9. Plant thorny shrubs.
10. Keep car or other vehicle keys securely locked away.
11. Install a deterrent alarm box.
12. Install a safe in the house.

With regard to point 10, if a criminal can break into a home and obtain the car keys to transport goods from the house using the homeowner's car, it is very unlikely that the vehicle will ever be recovered with little damage. It is highly likely that the vehicle will be burnt out to destroy evidence or will be passed on down the criminal channels with a new identity and false number plates. This is, therefore, a double trauma and hence the reason for safeguarding keys to any vehicles held at the home.

LEAVING HOME

Checklist for Going Away on Holiday

Before leaving home we should have a regime to ensure that we do not compromise our security. It is normal to close and lock all external doors and windows, even if we are only going out for a few minutes. We should also get into the routine of setting our intruder alarm and making sure that the side and/or

---

CHECKLIST FOR GOING AWAY ON HOLIDAY

- Cancel the milk and newspaper deliveries and ask a neighbour to check that this has been observed.
- Cut back shrubs and trees – make sure that intruders cannot hide behind foliage when you are away.
- Ensure that timers for lighting and other security devices or radios have been set and confirm that the electricity supply for these devices is available.
- Make sure that no valuables are on display – walk around the house and look through the windows.
- Ask a neighbour to collect the post.
- Try to have the neighbour park their car on your drive and to close curtains at night.
- Turn on any alarms or CCTV/observation system and confirm these are working correctly.
- Check that windows and doors are locked securely and make sure that the keys are put away securely.
- Put all tools away and out of sight.
- Ensure that the garage, garden shed and outbuildings are locked securely.
- Don't put your home address on luggage labels.
- Be aware, if using a taxi, of disclosing information to the driver or taxi company.
- Don't leave notes for visitors or neighbours on doors, etc. – these give information to criminals that the house is unoccupied.

Notes

---

back gate is locked. We must also lock our shed or garage and make sure that any valuables are not in sight.

Keys should be out of reach of letterboxes and, in the evening, we need to shut the curtains and leave some lights on. Car documents should not be left in the vehicle or ID put in obvious places, such as kitchens or hallways.

If we are going to be away for days or weeks at a time we need to take additional measures, such as cancelling newspaper and milk deliveries, and we need to consider asking our neighbours to close curtains, or park on our drive. Using a timer device to automatically turn lights and a radio on at night is also a good idea.

THE BUILDING REGULATIONS

In terms of the installation of security aids in and around the home we may want to ask ourselves what influence the Building Regulations can possibly have regarding the work we intend to perform. This same question also applies to the changes or modifications that we intend to make to the home. The Building Regulations were developed under powers provided in the Building Act 1984, and they apply in England and Wales. The current edition of the regulations is 'The Building Regulations 2000' (as amended). The majority of building projects are required to comply with them as they exist, to ensure the health and safety of people in and around all types of buildings, including the home. They also provide for energy conservation, and access to and the use of buildings.

The Building Regulations contain various sections dealing with definitions and procedures, including what is expected in terms of the technical performance of building work. They also define what types of projects amount to 'building work' and make these subject to control under the Building Regulations.

Anyone wanting to carry out building work that is subject to the Building Regulations is required by law to make sure it complies with the regulations and use a Building Control Service, which is normally that of the Local Authority or Council.

The primary responsibility for achieving compliance with the regulations rests with the person actually carrying out the building work. Therefore, if the homeowner is carrying out the

work personally, the responsibility will clearly be that of the homeowner. However, if you employ someone on your behalf, then the responsibility will be that of the person working for you.

A schedule contained in the Building Regulations groups a number of 'parts'. The particular 'parts' deal with individual aspects of building design and construction ranging from structural matters, safety and access to and use of buildings. These 'parts' set out the broad objectives or functions, which the individual aspects of the building design and construction must set out to achieve. They are therefore often referred to as 'functional requirements'. Practical guidance on ways to comply with the functional requirements in the Building Regulations is contained in a series of documents known as Approved Documents.

But just what influence can these regulations have for our security purposes? Professional advice should be sought before carrying out work in any area where we believe the Building Regulations can have an influence.

For instance, if we want to build or alter a garden wall to improve our home security, although the Building Regulations do not apply, the work must still be done with all provisions to ensure that it cannot cause accidents. Even then it must still be subject to Local Authority requirements to uphold the requirements for the local architecture to cover its material structure and size.

A further example is if we intend to replace the whole of the fixed frame and opening parts of windows in the home to improve our security, then the Building Regulations do actually apply. If the work is to our home and we employ a FENSA (Fenestration Self-Assessment Scheme) registered installer, we will not need to involve a Building Control Service because, on completion, the installer must give the local authority a certificate that the work complies with Part L and other appropriate parts of the Building Regulations. A certificate of compliance will be issued for their records.

An external window or door is a 'controlled fitting' under the Building Regulations and, as a result of this classification, these Regulations set out certain standards to be met when such a window or door needs to be replaced. When changing a window, the opening has to be of a size to provide at least the same potential for escape as the window it replaces. If replacing a main entry door, it is necessary to ensure that the threshold remains level for wheelchair users to have continued access to the home. These factors need to be considered when upgrading windows and doors for the reasons of security.

Part P of the Building Regulations is significant when it comes to electronic security and lighting systems, as it relates to electrical safety.

All new electrical work within a domestic setting must comply with Part P of the Building Regulations in England and Wales. This is legally enforceable. The normal way to achieve this is to apply British Standard BS 7671, known as the Wiring Regulations, including carrying out adequate inspection and testing to this standard of the completed works.

Under the new regulations, commencement of any work other than simple changes must be notified to the local building control and be performed by a 'competent person'. A competent person must be someone registered with a scheme that has been approved by the Department for Communities and Local Government (DCLG). In practice, therefore, the DIY person is restricted to the types of electrical work they can perform within the law in the domestic environment, with regard to main electrical circuits.

It is worth noting, however, that although the vast majority of electronic security systems are connected to, and do make use of, main electrical circuits as the primary supply source, most of the other control circuits work at lower safer voltages that are not subject to the same requirements. If changes are to be made within Part P, in terms of the 'competent persons' requirements and main electrical circuits, it would still remain the case that electrical safety must stay enshrined within the Building Regulations.

COUNCIL AND LOCAL AUTHORITY REQUIREMENTS

Local authorities, often also called councils, represent the government at a local level and through a leadership role they work to promote the social, economic and environmental well-being of their local areas and communities. This is through the external services they provide and influence. These include planning, advice and housing.

Therefore, the local authority does have an interest in security issues because of their influence on changes to the architecture of houses and their bordering areas. So, for instance, they do have a responsibility to control the construction and height of walls, fences and hedges, and so on. Beyond that they also enforce Acts in the local community. In terms of Acts that are important to security, the electronic security systems industry is affected by the Noise & Statutory Nuisance Act as far as audible alarms are concerned. So let us consider it in a little detail.

This Act makes provision for expenses incurred by the council and local authorities in abating or preventing the recurrence of a statutory nuisance to be a charge on the premises to which they relate. The Act also empowers an officer of the local authority to enter a premises by force, if need be, to silence an alarm if the operation of it is such as to give persons living or working in the vicinity reasonable cause for annoyance. This must follow an application made by the officer and accepted by a Justice of the Peace.

The strength of the Act is clear. In fact there are other governing codes that classify noise made by the operation of audible intruder alarms as a frequent cause of complaint. This relates mainly to duration rather than the volume of noise produced. Therefore, homeowners have a responsibility to ensure that a device fitted primarily for their own benefit does not become a nuisance to the public at large.

Environmental Protection Act 1990, Section 80, is used by the local authority to serve notice of the existence of noise amounting to a nuisance by the excessive sounding of an audible intruder alarm. Under this procedure the noise is classed as a statutory offence and subject on conviction to a heavy fine.

The 'Code of Practice on Noise from Audible Intruder Alarms' states the desirability of fitting automatic cut-out devices. These stop the sounder after a period of 20 minutes from activation of the system.

In order to ensure that any security system protecting the home cannot create noise amounting to a nuisance:

- Ensure that a reliable and well-maintained system is installed.
- False alarms must be non-existent or indeed controlled at the source.
- Confirm that the required automatic cut-out devices are incorporated and are programmed to a maximum time of 20 minutes.
- Give extra thought to silent signalling by remote communications.
- Remember that visual signalling devices, such as strobes, can continue after the 20-minute time period in order to continue to bring attention to the home.

COPING WITH A BURGLARY

A burglary can be a very upsetting experience, one that can often leave the victim feeling anxious about security and confused about what will happen next. In addition to the support the victim will receive from the local police, the national charity, Victim Support, provides free and confidential support to victims and witnesses of crime and their families.

If you think your home has been broken into, assess the situation carefully before taking action. If burglars are still there and you interrupt them, you could be at risk.

1. If you think the burglar is still in the property, or close by, this is an emergency. Call 999 and wait outside in a safe place for the police.
2. If you are sure the burglar has gone, this is not an emergency. Call your local police station.
3. Do not touch or move anything, especially where the burglars got in, or out, unless told to by the police.
4. When the police arrive, they will interview the victim and inspect the scene. Neighbours and other witnesses will be interviewed later. A Crime Reference Number will be raised, which will be required by the insurance company.
5. A forensic team may visit the home.
6. If a suspect is charged with the burglary of your home, you will be contacted by a Witness Care Unit or specialist department.
7. The Witness Care Unit will keep the victim updated about how the case is progressing through the criminal justice system until the case is closed. They will also give you information about attending court, should the victim need to.

chapter eight

Case Studies

In this the final chapter we will first look at some of the things burglars find attractive about a home when planning their activities. We will then turn our attention to some case studies for different premises, consider the fundamentals if we move to a new home and conclude by looking at the budgets associated with our security issues.

HOME FEATURES BURGLARS FIND ATTRACTIVE

Let us look at the ten things that have been recorded that most make a home attractive to a burglar. These things are historic, so they present interesting facts. They will also give us an overall idea of what we need to take into account when planning and implementing our security solutions.

1. A high front boundary.
2. Low side and rear boundaries.
3. Wheelie bins accessible.
4. No visible intruder alarm.
5. No security lighting.
6. Valuables on display.
7. Open or unsecured windows.
8. Unsecured garage door.
9. Unlocked shed.
10. Paved path or driveway.

TYPICAL CASE STUDIES

We are now able to recall case studies for three main home types. These case studies will give

us an indication of how we can plan our security for such typical homes.

These are generically planned security solutions because it cannot be the case that two houses are identical or that the needs of different individuals can ever be exactly the same.

The homes that follow show the particular considerations with which they are faced and are:

- A bungalow.
- A house of two or more storeys.
- An apartment in a gated community.

The particular considerations below follow the sequence in which they have been covered in this book. The other additional and more general security aspects and considerations that need to be dealt with for any home can be found by referring to the appropriate chapters.

A Bungalow

General

Bungalows have all of their rooms on one level (including bedrooms that may hold valuables), so some of the important rooms of these homes can be more easily concealed by shrubs and fences, etc. Therefore, these perimeter features should not be of excess height or the bungalow will be more hidden and vulnerable.

Dealing with Bogus Callers

Since all of the rooms are on one level, bogus callers who target bungalows can more easily look into all of the rooms of the home in advance of making a call to the premises. They may also try to establish who is in the bungalow at the time before calling.

There is also, relative to the size of the bungalow, more access points for sneak thieves to enter than a similar size house with more than one storey.

Physical Security Measures

Bungalows are rarely targeted by burglars during the night when the occupants are asleep, unless the burglars are hardened criminals. This is because the occupants are on the same floor of the house and they can react quicker in the event they detect the burglar. However, bungalows do tend to have many access points, including bedrooms, so the physical security restraints, such as doors, windows, shutters, grilles, locks and locking devices, all need special attention.

Safes and visible and perimeter deterrents should be selected as appropriate for the risk.

Electronic Security Systems

Intruder alarms as a minimum should offer volumetric protection by PIRs for the hallway, if vulnerable, the main bedroom and main living areas. Other rooms that are vulnerable to attack, hold valuables or are not overlooked by other properties should also be protected by PIRs. Alarm contacts should be used on all external doors.

Intercoms, door entry or call systems could be installed, if appropriate to the specific premises or needs of the individual. An observation system in kit form with up to eight cameras, and using an LCD monitor for viewing at home, would be appropriate. Remote viewing could also be set up using a universal plug 'n' play auto network configuration.

Fire detection should be included throughout the hallway and carbon monoxide detection, if appropriate.

Lighting for Security

Lighting used externally can be more easily attacked at ground level so luminaires with robust housings are needed, or columns or posts should be used to make the lighting more difficult to

reach. Cables are best concealed or buried.

Detection devices used for demand lighting need to be inaccessible, so these are also best mounted on columns or posts.

System Signalling and Self-Contained Security Devices

Attention must be given to installing signalling devices, such as external sounders, at positions where it is more difficult for them to be reached. Use the peaks of the home or chimney stacks, where possible. Alternatively, columns or posts may be needed if high security is a requirement.

Additional hidden external audible signalling devices can be used by concealing them behind vents or air bricks.

Telephone lines used for signalling need to be hidden, protected or monitored.

The need for key-holders, home automation or any miscellaneous self-contained security devices, as appropriate to the specific bungalow.

A House of Two or More Storeys
General

In general, the ground floor will be the most vulnerable and the first point of attack by burglars, as using climbing aids to reach higher floors presents difficulties. Houses with upstairs bedrooms may still be subject to burglary by determined criminals during the night, if the occupants are asleep upstairs.

Dealing with Bogus Callers

Bogus callers may assess the quality and size of the house before calling. They might try to obtain information with respect to the occupants in terms of ages and the numbers of persons living on the premises in advance of making any approach. Therefore, the bogus caller may be selective in terms of the time they call, taking into account they want to target a vulnerable person when in the home alone.

Physical Security Measures

The ground floor should receive most attention when assessing the physical security measures.

Beware of flat roofs on ground-floor rooms or on garages, if they give access to first-floor landing windows, as these openings also need protection.

Safes and visible and perimeter deterrents should be selected as appropriate for the risk.

Electronic Security Systems

Intruder alarms as a minimum should offer volumetric protection by PIRs for the hallway, if it is vulnerable, and for the main living areas. Any other rooms that are vulnerable to attack, hold valuables or are not overlooked by other properties, should also be protected by PIRs. Landings should also be protected by PIRs with a facility to switch off at night, if these landings lead to bedrooms. Alarm contacts should be used on all external doors.

Intercoms, door entry and call systems, should be installed, as appropriate to the specific premises or needs of the individual. An observation system in kit form with up to eight cameras and using an LCD monitor for viewing at home would be appropriate. Remote viewing could also be set up using a universal plug 'n' play auto network configuration. Any security-related components used externally, such as alarm signalling equipment or cameras, should be installed at a high elevation, ideally at roof height.

Fire detection should be included throughout the hallway and landings, and carbon monoxide detection, if appropriate

Lighting for Security

Lighting components used externally can be installed at roof level to improve security by making the component parts more difficult to reach.

Detection devices used for demand lighting can also be fitted out of reach.

System Signalling and Self-Contained Security Devices

Signalling devices, such as external sounders, can always be sited at higher points, making them more difficult to attack.

Telephone lines used for signalling may also be better protected by installing at high elevations.

The need for key-holders, home automation or any miscellaneous self-contained security devices as appropriate to the specific house.

An Apartment in a Gated Community

General

These can be very difficult targets for the criminal, if the neighbours are reliable and respectable. They receive the protection of other near neighbours, unless those neighbours are themselves criminals who may provide information to others.

Dealing with Bogus Callers

Bogus callers will need to get access through the gates to make cold calls and through any perimeter gates and community doors. The bogus caller may also feel trapped when inside the main apartment building, which is something they always try to avoid.

Physical Security Measures

In general, the physical security measures tend to be good on quality gated communities, with special locks and strong access doors. There are particular requirements if physical security products and devices are being specified for dwelling entrance doors in residential buildings and, in particular, above ground level. Locking must be designed for easy operation when opening and closing entrance doors, and the architecture of the building must account for this. It is also possible, depending on the floor lived in, that access to windows is very difficult, so this further improves security.

Electronic Security Systems

Intruder alarms can benefit these developments with alarm contacts on the main doors specific to the apartment and a PIR in any special room holding valuables.

Intercoms, door entry, call systems, CCTV and observation systems are normally installed during the development of the premises, so are expected to be of high security and appropriate to the quality of the development.

Fire detection will be included in the complex as appropriate.

Lighting for Security

External lighting will be included in the complex, as appropriate, but internal lighting can be modified to suit the needs of the individual.

System Signalling and Self-Contained Security Devices

Signalling devices, such as external sounders, can always be sited where they are difficult to be reached.

Telephone lines used for signalling may not be visible on the outside of the apartment, which is a distinct advantage.

The use of a number of key-holders will normally be easier to organize due to the closeness of other neighbours. Home automation or any miscellaneous self-contained security devices, as appropriate to the specific house. Door viewers are often fitted as standard on apartment doors. Limiters may also be fitted to allow the door to be securely held ajar whilst the homeowner checks the credentials of a caller.

Conclusions

Each case study includes the use of an electronic security system comprising an intruder alarm because it is this technology that forms the nucleus of electronic security. In each case it employed passive infra-red (PIR) detectors as protective devices but the number of these sensors used and their positioning will always depend on the particular home.

Remember that we always dedicate our main protection to the ground floor of any house, as this floor is always the most vulnerable.

A good option would be to use an observation kit as these are easy to install for domestic purposes and they include purpose-designed parts, so all components are compatible and their connections are clearly defined. Dome cameras are popular for the home market. Domes can be used externally on the house if they are specified for such a purpose and have weatherproof housings. For the larger home, and if internal cameras are required, mini-domes can be installed and, as these are particularly small, they do not have an overbearing appearance.

In the case studies discussed, both the bungalow and the house of two or more storeys

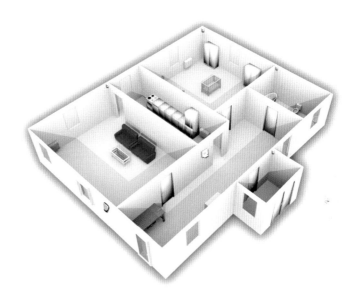

As a home layout ground-floor example, it would be best to site the control panel keypad in the main hallway because it is the most convenient position for the system user, and then protect this with a PIR in the same area. Other PIRs could be sited in all rooms other than the bathroom because of the problems that would be caused there with humidity.

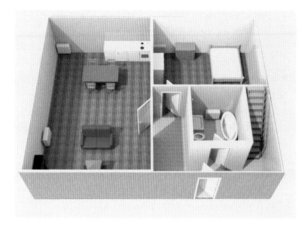

Representative of a ground-floor home layout example. We could do the same thing but also use a PIR to protect the first-floor landing. Other detectors could be added to other first-floor areas or additional rooms, as required.

could be detached, semi-detached or terraced. This means that they could be influenced by near neigbours, in the same way as the apartment in a gated community. Equally they could be on housing estates or in city centre settings.

We now have many old but very large farm buildings being converted into a number of rural residential properties with shared courtyards, so these are also influenced by near neighbours. On the other hand, certain homes are very much alone in remote settings with only distant neighbours.

All of these settings do have some effect on the measures we need to put in place when considering our security. There are advantages and disadvantages with all settings. So with that

in mind, consider the main impact of the setting on a property (see box opposite).

A concluding thought to all of our investigations must be that with all the will in the world, we can never live without some form of security.

It is fair to add that no matter what level or degree of security we decide to put in place, it must, by its very nature, offer us some degree of controlling influence to the problems of crime we must surely always face.

Let us now give some thought to moving to a new home, which may already have reasonable levels of security fitted.

MOVING TO A NEW HOME

If we were to move to a new home that had little in the way of security aids fitted, then we could easily start with an open mind and upgrade its security. However, if we were to move to a new home that already featured a good variety of security aids, we would probably only need to customize them for our own purposes.

So let us give a little thought as to what we may, or may not, need to do and look at some worst-case scenarios for the main areas:

- **Home risk assessment.** In the first instance, carry out your home risk assessment and record the findings.
- **Physical security.** The keys for external locks and locking devices would need to be changed if we were genuinely concerned that the previous owner of the house could compromise our security by still having duplicate copies in their possession.
- **Electronic security systems**
  - The setting codes would need to be changed.

Observation kit with a single camera kit using a dome camera.

GUIDE TO THE SECURITY OF RESIDENTIAL HOME SETTINGS

Homes with Near Neighbours

- Many homeowners are only comfortable knowing they have others around them and feel more secure and safe in the presence of others.
- Key-holders can reside closer to the protected home.
- The closeness of other people helps the implementation of 'neighbourhood watch' schemes.
- More observers are available to witness activities around the house.
- Observers can also respond quickly to alarm-activations.
- Opportunists actually have more chances to target homes with near neighbours. This is because in areas with a high density of neighbours, they can mingle with the local population more easily.
- Barriers such as fences and boundaries may be shared with other houses. Near neighbours may also be careless in leaving climbing aids and tools unprotected which could be of benefit to criminals.
- The homeowners' security may be compromised by the lack of maintenance employed by near neighbours to shared facilities. The homeowner can never be totally independent when there are near neighbours.

Homes in Remote Settings with Only Distant Neighbours

- Certain homeowners want to live in more private, remote environments and are prepared to implement the security measures to cater for this.
- Homeowners can use more diverse security measures, such as guard dogs, that would be unwelcome in normal residential areas with a high-density population.
- Criminals may be prepared to use more force in remote areas believing that persons living in such environments may be wealthy and in particular if a lack of security around the home is suspected.
- The distance that the emergency services must travel can be a disadvantage.
- Criminals have more time to flee from the area relative to the remoteness.
- The lack of close neighbours as observers can present an easier and earlier opportunity for criminals to spend time overcoming the perimeter protection.
- Criminals must be restricted by the perimeter protective measures or be detected at an early stage.
- Provisions may need to be taken to cater for any mains failure at the home, as houses in remote locations are vulnerable during power outages.
- The lighting and electronic security systems need to be given special attention when considering power failures.
- Only remote signalling can benefit electronic security systems as local (audible) signalling is of little value to those properties that have no close neighbours or see many passers-by.
- The signalling from any remote signalling would need to be highly secure and may need dual communications, i.e. by both landline and radio links to support each other.

- It is possible that zones and attributes would also have to be altered if the systems were to be used differently by the new owner.
- Any signalling to remote points would need changing, as key-holders would almost certainly be different.
- Give some thought as to how a response to any alarm-activation would be achieved.

- It would not normally be the case that the previous owner would take away equipment. However, if this were to happen it is always possible to retrofit new equipment using the existing cabling.
- **Lighting**
  - The lighting may only need updating to energy efficient providing it was

traditional but otherwise was already offering good security and in good repair.

- Give some thought to the use of timers and photocells, and adapt your internal lighting to suit your own preferences.

It may also be the case that we are considering moving to a new house. Before carrying out a move, it is always wise to do a little research and ask a few questions, such as:

Q. What is the history of crime in the neighbourhood?

Also check the other areas it borders with to see if they have a history of crime that could begin to extend to the other surrounding areas.

Q. Are the homeowners moving because they have actually been subject to crime?

Even if not, have the owners ever lived in fear of it?

Q. Can arrangements be made to have key-holders available convenient to the new home?

A response to any alarm signal will be required to take appropriate action.

Q. Is access to the area in which the new home is sited easy for criminals?

Check to see if any neighbourhood watch is in operation or any community gating is in existence to watch for suspicious activities.

Q. What is the state of the telephone lines?

This will govern the ability for remote communications to be effective.

In terms of the future, when moving to a new home I suppose we will see a constant progression with the security and quality of our physical openings, such as windows and doors and the strength of our locking devices. We will probably see more activity by sneak thieves as our physical security develops but this will be countered by a greater use of CCTV and observation systems with images being increasingly sent over the internet and on to new-generation mobile phones. We will see a much greater use of intercoms as a replacement for door bells, so that callers to a house can be better interrogated from a more distant point by those within the property.

But let us now look at the overall price of security as it stands at present.

SECURITY BUDGETS

Can we really put an exact price on the security we want to implement in order to protect ourselves, our family and our possessions? Probably not, is the answer. This is because the importance of security to every individual is different and everyone has different priorities. Also, it would be difficult to know where it all starts and where it all ends. However we can say that, to some extent or another, we can all improve our security without spending a fortune. At the end of the day it is all down to what we are able to spend and what we are happy to spend to obtain peace of mind. Balanced against this we also need to take into account any legal or insurers' requirements.

We may also ask the question as to how much practical work we can carry out ourselves. This question, in the main, needs to be answered by ourselves because the answer largely lies in our own DIY or practical skills. But there is still more to it than that! As an example, electrical work is certainly a problem because of legislation but simple plug-in electrical devices cause no difficulties. Also, no inexperienced person can contemplate working on automatic gates and such because of the onerous safety requirements. However, we have a multitude of devices that can be installed by competent DIY people, such as small locking devices. So there are areas in which we can help ourselves in terms of budgets and cost-savings.

What we do need to know though is what is available in terms of overall security and I genuinely hope this book will have given every reader some scope for thought, so that improvements can be made to safeguard each and everyone's welfare at a realistic cost. I suppose that certain things, such as awareness, do not even cost anything. Indeed some people in their own minds are quite happy to rely on window blinds and obstructions on window shelves to deter intruders from attempting to break into their homes, although, of course, most of us are prepared to invest rather more when it comes to the physical security protection of our homes.

It is not the case that I can put exact monetary figures on any particular thing because the parameters for different systems and issues vary enormously. We need to think of the benefits and costs with a clear mind. For instance, should we invest a lot of money in security lighting, which may be an excellent security aid at night but would have little impact during the day, so could the money be better spent elsewhere on other security measures? As a further example, we may find that a home fitted with new-generation external intruder alarm boxes will visually illustrate to the observer that a good investment has been made in security.

However, the burglar will never know the extent of the detection devices that have been installed in the house, so will be very reluctant to target the premises. Therefore, we can budget sensibly for the size of the system to be fitted, as it need not be overstretched providing the information regarding its size and capacity is not disclosed.

Do not forget that lighting for security purposes does have a running cost in terms of electrical energy, so always think about using low-energy lamps. Indeed all electronic security systems do have associated running costs but it is fair to say that these are relatively inexpensive. However, once again do not overlook the costs of running any chosen system and the maintenance that is required of it.

For those of us who want to consider entering a contract with a recognized installation company specializing in electronic security, then we may wish to consider a remotely monitored system that covers the main technologies, such as intruder and fire detection. These are paid monthly, so can be easily budgeted for, as the ongoing costs, including maintenance, monitoring and any repairs, are clearly defined. The equipment tends to remain the property of the installation company and is only subject to a rental contract.

We should always try to incorporate any forms of our security into the general features of the house as best we can. In other words, if we are going to install hedges, fences, gates and such, let them perform dual roles by giving some thought to both the aesthetics and the security. Select hedges that look good but are not of excessive height and cannot conceal villains. Choose fences and gates that improve our home but are not solid, so do not let criminals hide within the boundaries they serve.

If we are going to install security systems, make sure they are of time-honoured format and are user-friendly, so are not a burden or a grudge purchase, otherwise we may become reluctant to use them regularly. They must be convenient and installed to give reliable performance and yet reflect future trends. Also, make sure that any potential problems with the proposed installation at the home are addressed so as to avoid any difficulties at the actual time of fitting.

Remember that the whole idea of carrying out the home risk assessment is to overview security with a view to updating it and being alert as to what we have or may need. The logic of giving it a grade is in the understanding that different criminals target different properties. Burglars do not want a challenge, so prefer soft targets. If we visibly improve our security, burglars will be discouraged from attacking our homes. Such improvements will not suggest to burglars that we have only done so because we have recently acquired more valuables and are trying to protect these valuables: in practice, we all have things that other people may wish to steal. We do not want to become victims of these criminals by letting our possessions be taken from us lightly.

Give some thought to what could go wrong and what would be the result if you moved

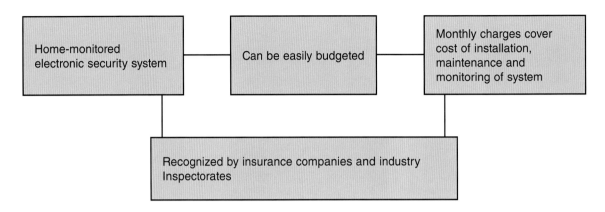

Home-monitored security systems. Budget.

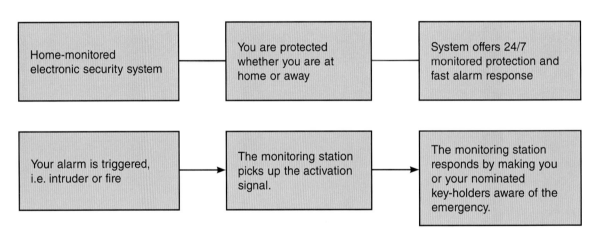

Home-monitored security systems. Operation.

home. Could you pass on the cost of the security to the new owner? Otherwise, could you take the security with you such as that offered by stand-alone or radio devices that do not have interconnecting wires or cables?

Think of security and convenience. A prime example is an intercom. These are much more convenient for the homeowner than a door bell, as it enables callers to be interrogated from a remote point rather than the homeowner having to actually go to the door to check who the caller is. Think of progression and the modern age because as the saying goes 'people who live in the past die in the past'.

In conclusion I can only say that in the real world crime will never disappear, and therefore it is up to us to as individuals to look at the results of our risk assessment and to then move forward in a responsible way.

Constructive and effective security need not be too expensive.

Glossary

ABC of risk The Area and Boundaries/Buildings and Contents assessed in relation to the risk of a property.

Automatic lighting systems Lighting systems that do not need to be turned on and off manually.

Bogus callers Those who may not attempt to break into homes but will try to trick or con their way in.

Building Regulations Regulations that contain various sections dealing with definitions and procedures including what is expected in terms of the technical performance of building work.

Burglary A person is said to be guilty of burglary if they enter any building or part of a building as a trespasser and steal or have an intention to steal, inflict grievous bodily harm or to do unlawful damage to the building or anything in it.

Call systems Electronic security systems that allow a user to produce an electronic call for help.

CCTV and observation systems Systems used to capture, record and playback video images.

Demand lighting systems Lighting operated only for short periods of time.

Distraction and artifice burglary Burglary carried out by trickery or by distracting techniques.

Door viewer A device used to be able to see a caller to the home before opening the door to them.

Extended period lighting Lighting kept on for a long period normally from dusk to dawn.

Home automation A technique of automating systems within the home so that those systems will then be automatically controlled to include security alongside energy management.

Home risk assessment A systematic method of looking at all of our home security issues and considering the problems we could be faced with associated with the individual or property to be protected.

Intercoms and door entry Systems used to interrogate callers or with a view to allow authorized callers to enter the home.

Intruder alarms Electronic systems used to detect intrusion originally known as burglar alarms.

Key-holders Persons authorized to look after a home and holding keys to the premises.

Local signalling Security signalling, such as sounders and strobes/beacons, that only provide notification of an event close to the protected home.

Low-energy lighting Lighting that in relative terms is inexpensive to run.

Luminaire A compete lighting assembly including the bulb and enclosure.

Mortise/mortice lock A lock that is installed flush on the surface of the area it protects. These provide good qualities of strength.

Perimeter security The security measures that protect the outskirts or external fabric of a home.

Physical security The solid restraints or barriers that can be natural or man-made and are used for security.

Remote signalling Security signalling that provides notification of an event to a remote point normally over telephone lines or by radio frequency.

Rim lock A lock that is installed on the surface of the area it protects. These are not as strong as equivalent mortise locks.

Security grade The level of risk to security that will be a grade somewhere in the range from low through to high.

Self-contained security devices Security components that are not connected to any other device or system. Examples are small switches on doors that respond to a door being opened.

Sneak thieves Use sneak tactics to gain entry into the home rather than using violence or force.

Wireless systems Electronic systems that do not have cables or wires but use a free space form of transmission such as radio signals.

Useful Contacts

The first line of information for security issues should always be through your local police authority. However, beyond the scope of the local police there are many other services available that are related to security help and support.

We are only providing the most prominent and useful contacts because links through these can be made to obtain more specific lines of help and assistance:

In an emergency

call 999

Metropolitan Police Service

www.met.police.uk/

Crime prevention

0300 123 1212

Neighbourhood Watch

www.neighbourhoodwatch.net
0116 2710052 (office hours)

Immobilise

www.immobilise.com

Home Office

www.homeoffice.gov.uk

Crimestoppers

If you have information about a crime but would prefer not to speak to police, you can call Crimestoppers anonymously on 0800 555 111. Crimestoppers is an independent charity: www. crimestoppers-uk.org

Victim Support

www.victimsupport.org.uk
or contact the victim support line on: 0845 30 30 900

INDUSTRY REGULATORY AUTHORITIES

There are a number of bodies that regulate or have a prominent role in the security industry. These exist to ensure that high standards are upheld and are consistent. They are also responsible for those policies or inspection practices that influence home security issues.

Some of the most important authorities follow:

Association of British Insurers (ABI)

The UK's leading financial services trade association and responsible for insurance risks underwriting.

Association of Chief Police Officers (ACPO)

They bring together the expertise and experience of Chief Police Officers from England, Wales and Northern Ireland and prepare policies used within the security industry including those that have an influence in the home sector.

British Security Industry Association (BSIA)

The trade association for the professional security industry and dedicated to upholding high standards.

Fencing Contractors Association (FCA)

A trade association having a membership including fencing contractors, material/product manufacturers and suppliers.

Fenestration Self-Assessment Scheme (FENSA)

Set up by the Glass and Glazing Federation in response to Building Regulations for double glazing companies in England and Wales.

Fire Industry Association (FIA)

Promotes the professional status of the UK fire safety industry.

Master Locksmiths Association (MLA)

The principal trade body representing locksmiths and promoting standards within the industry.

National Approvals Council for Security Systems (NACOSS)

An independent supervisory body that exists to ensure member bodies comply with industry standards and codes of practice.

National Security Inspectorate (NSI)

The specialist approvals and certification body that inspects companies providing home security plus business security and fire safety services.

United Kingdom Accreditation Service (UKAS)

The national accreditation body recognized by the government to assess against internationally agreed standards organizations that provide certification, testing, inspection and calibration services.

Security Industry Authority (SIA)

The organization responsible for regulating the private security industry in the UK and managing the voluntary Approved Contractor Scheme which measures private security suppliers.

Security Systems and Alarms Inspection Board (SSAIB)

A prominent certification body that offers a wide range of schemes for electronic security system installers and guarding security services in the UK.

Index